Perfectionism

Proven Strategies to End Procrastination Accept Yourself

(How to Let Go of Self-criticism Build Self-esteem and Find Balance)

Stuart Collins

Published By **Ryan Princeton**

Stuart Collins

All Rights Reserved

Perfectionism: Proven Strategies to End Procrastination Accept Yourself (How to Let Go of Self-criticism Build Self-esteem and Find Balance)

ISBN   978-1-998038-38-1

Legal & Disclaimer

The information contained in this book is not designed to replace or take the place of any form of medicine or professional medical advice. The information in this book has been provided for educational & entertainment purposes only.

The information contained in this book has been compiled from sources deemed reliable, and it is accurate to the best of the Author's knowledge; however, the Author cannot guarantee its accuracy and validity and cannot be held liable for any errors or omissions. Changes are periodically made to this book. You must consult your doctor or get professional medical advice before using any of the suggested remedies, techniques, or information in this book.

Table Of Contents

Chapter 1: Do Something Without Fear.

The world has been repeatedly confronted with concerns about the development of the globe. It went from a place of stagnation, to one of disorder. When we examine the history of mankind we will see the petty mistakes that civilizations did by refusing to accept the need to take action. Perhaps one of the most terrifying human rights violations which the world has seen as the Holocaust that was initiated by Nazi Germany that included genocide that was committed against a total of Six millions of European Jews during the Second World War even though there was a lot of planning going on prior to the outbreak of the Second World War. This is an abominable act not to mention a terrible crime as well as another that humanity has nothing to contribute to. How come world leaders have refused to accept the leadership flag and end the calamity caused by the Holocaust? The decision was made early in a potential life span of six million people and likely million even more?

According to me, there was a component of fear. And it was the anxiety of taking actions that eventually exploded the amount of violence, and led to a huge global war which no one had witnessed before from. It is a question that we should consider is: how do we stop the behavior of elimination of fear in our societies? How can we build a culture not only that of self-confidence, but also a determination to spread democratic freedom? How do we foster the qualities of leadership in ourselves, in order that, with respect and humility to stand up for our beliefs?

Many leaders believe they're here on earth to contribute to an improvement. To be a an active participant in a positive transformation it is essential to be free from being frightened. It is impossible to progress if he believes that the change will not be successful. If you are able to improve the positive elements of your psychological state it is essential to assume your permanent responsibility to achieve the goals of wellness. It is important to have wins throughout the process to keep the trust of others and inspires a sense of and a desire to do greater. In the absence of the rewards that come with the achievement of a milestone that is progressive and a challenge to keep your focus on the projects to prioritize and can be difficult to remain healthy physical and mental well-being. It is important not to avoid defeat when your desires are not true; you must be able to establish trust on yourself as well as those whom you're dating.

It is important to keep in mind that being able of being able to hear others, and also to pay attention to their own thoughts is an ability that many are aspiring to lose. Being able to perform can bring about success. the success of those who want to join the overall management. They will be looking to be members of their group of managers based on principles of honesty, trust as well as respect and dignity. The people want to work in an organization that encourages relationships and modernization. They want to work with an individual leader who is able to lead without tension and who can influence by using persuading language. This creates confidence, positivity, as well as the capability to create change with positive outcomes.

Beating the fear of failure is the initial step towards the path to success. Therefore, you should reduce the fear of loss; as fears of failing will trigger anxiety and doubts regarding the ability of a person and their capacity to manage. If you are a leader, it is likely that there will be those who remain ready to criticize you for what's not right, instead of those who claim this is a major event and we'll have an more memorable event next year. Leaders constantly fight to protect people who feel jealous of the achievements made and want to figure out an opportunity to attain the satisfaction of success without the work required. The successful leaders have to face fears at one moment or another. So they understand how to battle anxiety. They know is the best method to reduce anxiety is to fight those that will require conduct a thorough communications strategy to stop the gradual changes while ensuring that positive and robust conversations will result in Resolutions, and Permanent resolutions.

From indecision to taking action

It's officially summer in the desert of high elevation. The snow was on the watermelons in the morning. The sun is shining brightly however, I'm frigid. The oven has been turned off and the boys are returning this morning for their third time during the week. The house we live in is just 2 years old. it is believed it was hit by lightning. It is a common occurrence in northwestern New Mexico, they say that they visit him regularly. But, I am thankful for the beautiful house I live in and know that it'll soon be the time when temperatures return to each room.

However, it's not always an easy issue, which can be solved with a telephone visit, a call or an enormous bill to easily be settled. Certain situations or circumstances require more thought and more stressful. There are people I know who aren't taking their job seriously and worry that they might losing them. There are family and friends of mine relatives who face many financial difficulties and, just like most Americans currently, struggle to make their mortgage payments and the minimum amount due on their credit card.

In the course of my time, I've had executive roles. After my racing days in high school, I attended school to college, and then onto further education, as well as "great people jobs". Through the years I've heard about secrets and tales, and have been a participant in the challenges and joys of my coworkers. In my current life I realize that I don't want to become the manager anymore. In fact, I don't wish to be a slave with someone else, which could result in unintentionally a pig or even worse, what is more restrictive on choices. Therefore, having your own company is the best option. Also, having an online marketing, I am able to be part of an "team". So, they always possess "visions" with which they can share information, help and guidance. However, the distinction is that I'm not accountable for their accomplishments but they are. I enjoy leading and encourage people to follow an unifying vision, however I don't want to be held responsible to their performance. It can make a significant change, and though this is liberating for me from responsibility, it could also mean giving them the power.

Learning is among the most exciting aspects that comes with developing technology. If other people could create the vision of what's feasible, it could provide a powerful incentive. In the morning, I thought about the numerous exercises and webinars I've enjoyed. I was thinking of the words of John Jackson, "More people fail because of a hesitant heart." He spoke about getting rid of being caught in the "paralysis of analysis" and in encouraging people to put forth efforts, but the decision was made to act. That's the essence. The book's conclusion, Robert Kiyosaki's novel, Father Rich, poor father, it states, "Do not play safe today, be smart, act!"

There is no unreserved heart. However, I do have the "zeal for a new conversion" and would like to help others share their opportunities. But, bold actions aren't for everyone. Many people aren't essential. People have a hard time making choices and taking actions. They stammer and bend over apologize as well as "yes, but" every chance, but ultimately they fail many opportunities. It is heartbreaking, since our greatest satisfaction often occurs when we face one of the toughest problems. I am reminded of the saying that goes, "You can take a horse in the water, but you cannot poo drink it." I saw this happen with my horses as well as witnessed him playing with a few colleagues. It's true, "Look before you jump," be sure not to appear stupefied.

Indecision and fear is a challenge to overcome. The definition of risk-taking is a risk that involves uncertainty. But, the shift between doubt and decision-making is achievable once one is willing and eager to alter. If you're willing, as long as you're in control and a strong support system an alteration is possible. Recognize the fears and decide to act. It is not necessary to be aware of each step prior to you can begin. It is essential to be prepared to complete the first task before proceeding to the next step and the following.

Locate a mentor or an experienced person who is who is involved in the same activities you'd like to get involved in. Decide to embark on the new you with a bright future, and get started on becoming the best you can be. Whatever you have in mind, figure out ways to live the moment you first saw it.

It is for this reason that just a fraction of people have an entrepreneurial mindset. Fear can be a very powerful factor that is increased in our culture. Recently, I was told by a friend, "You know I was looking for a change, now I just need eggs!" It's an excellent overview of the way people worry about starting an undertaking that is big, exciting and fresh. They require crowns and long-lasting chance. Remember the possibility of doing something by yourself. You don't have to do everything by yourself.

Since I am passionate about all things that is achievable, I want to could feel all the joy and inspiration emotions and joy which comes from helping people and the transfer of "copy and paste" directly into the fear of every day life, to find the heart. I'd like to type "ctrl c" then "ctrl v" on the heart's keyboard to ensure that love and love will take over anxiety, and an open heart is transformed and becomes active.

Make your dreams come true without fear

The trick is to transform your goals into reality, despite the worries. What we must get is to find the device that takes us into a whole new realm free of anxiety.

In order to live life fully it is essential to manage the fears that we have, conquer those fears, and tell a great narrative about these fears. A fear of failure could be one of the main fears that keeps the majority of us from taking chances. We don't want to put our trust in others as well as our company or funds. The majority of people prefer to be in a safe place and not be concerned about any tragedies or failures that happen in their lives. But, how do be successful within a world that is populated by anxiety?

The very first option is to control your fear. When we look around there are numerous brave individuals. They're not scared and not just because they've never had fear in their own lives, but due to the fact that they've learned how to conquer their fear. If, for instance, they were hesitant to stand in front of a crowd and wanted to speak in public, they'd give talks until they felt comfortable speaking. In the event that they were hesitant to go back to their work and even though they weren't completely satisfied, they were successful. High achievers recognize anxiety in their lives, and strive to be fearless, regardless of the fear.

Below are some easy steps to help you conquer the fear and help you realize your goals.

Recognize your own fears

Instead of shredding your anxiety beneath the rug without acknowledging the existence of your fears get yourself a little more brave and master the art of managing the situation. Put them out instead of hiding them in the sand. See directly in your eyes the fearful gaze, and talk about it openly. Find out how you can manage your anxiety as you discover that a lot of your anxieties that are based on your head are not true.

Accept that your fears are normal.

It's common and ok to experience fears and you should accept the fact that your anxieties are there because of a reason. The fear of being afraid can alert us to the fact that it is necessary to be cautious and assist us in avoiding risk. But, it is important to determine how rational the fears are and whether or not there any logic behind it. This way we will be able to determine how serious the risk is and the risk involved and whether or not we need to trust or not.

Find out the root of your anxiety.

Find out the root of your anxiety and understand what it is that causes it. This will allow you to identify your fears in a clear way which is often quite different from the initial believed. Be aware of the limits imposed by your fears and decide whether it's worth every moment for fears. Then you will realize that your anxiety is not quite as bad as it appears.

Be confident and think without fear

It is possible to dream without anxiety. Consider how you'd act even if you didn't exist. Return to your own day and reflect on the occasions where you achieved success and won, regardless of the fear was present. Make a tiny step towards the right direction and begin to be able to face the fear of being afraid. After you've accepted the reality of your fear, you're now to step outside of your comfort zone. Gain the self-confidence necessary to face your fears, and then find the confidence to take on the task you've been given to take on.

The majority of us don't live a full life, so we get caught in our own anxieties and abandon the goals we have set for ourselves. Every day we experience these occasions in the form of "EUREKA" sometimes in life however we don't always realize this because we're preoccupied with our anxieties. Fear of failing deters our from taking on new paths. The fear of being uncertain keeps our feet, and our goals as low as we would like. It is, however, more beneficial to strive to be successful instead of living and feel like you're not trying even once.

If you think that the fears you had are no longer there and you begin to manage your fears, you'll build a positive faith system. You will no longer be involved to transforming these thoughts to words and those phrases into actions. These actions won't be influenced by anxiety or negative feelings. You will soon be applauded by your peers for the way you incorporate your values in your words, actions and even the reality of your life to reach the goal you set.

Don't waste time speaking about your dream. Instead, get out there and pursue your goals of achieving the life you've always wanted. The man spends a lot of time thinking about his hopes and strategies, as well as how to face his challenges. It is time to take these thoughts into practice. Break those chains of fear that hinder you from pursuing your life to the fullest.

A verb is to be taken

It is a verb. Do your best to live life with action not in your mind. Picasso declared: "Action is the key to success." Don't believe me, but your mind is a gorgeous one, and we recognize the effects in the event that we do not use it. Thought cannot force us to leap over the boundaries of our fear and into the unknown in the opposite is designed to convince our minds from taking a leap of faith. A leap of faith that is a leap with absolute confidence that we're bound to be landing on our feet, somewhere in between that actual step before shots are dropped onto the floor it is evident. It opens many possibilities and opportunities that one could only think of sitting on its own.

There is a gorgeous soul quote in my bulletin board. It's a quote I'd love if could identify the person who is one of my everyday guides. "When you reach the limit of everything you know, you have to believe that you will be given to walk or wings to fly." The images of the cliff, and playing the sport of wings provide me the strength to go on in peace, without trepidation and to live with a great deal of enthusiasm. The image of the cliff fills me with hope and gives me the confidence of knowing that everything will be fine every day.

I was a huge fan of leaping whenever I was young I jumped all the time, and made use of many occasions that appeared to be a little crazy to my siblings and parents as well as my parents. My followers knew that I was an incredibly brave actor from the local scene and I have to declare that I loved the awe. The faith that I had at the time, that faith which we are all born, let me play with tricks that could harm me if I stopped contemplating my intentions to achieve. There is no discussion of broken arms or dark eye. The thing is, I was not able to think about it; I believed it was an exciting adventure, so I followed my passion into the depths of excitement.

The faith I experienced at the time is the same faith I have now, when my fears were sucked up by the experiences of life and exhausted state of my mind brought the voice of my self-centered ego into my heart. I discovered that I could stop that voice and recognize the fact that it was trying to save me, and then allow my eyes to see the things that bring me satisfaction. It's a moment of magic in which we are aware that the choices we make can lead to an perspective of our own and shows the world what we're capable of.

It's an unavoidable habit that they haven't lost as they transition from childhood to adulthood for example, Steve Irwin is a great instance. Even though his death came sooner than most of us would have thought I firmly believe in him. Will not settle for a different way of living. A life of high quality lived up to the very end does not have a measurement in the time. We all create our lives here with the same way and I've been looking for these. They encourage me and validate my work. When you stop and pay attention to them, you'll see them also. A 71-year-old grandmother from Oregon that lost her sight at age of 20 experienced a dramatic jump in her very first attempt at skydiving. When asked what she thought of it when she was asked, she responded, "Oh, the only word I have in heaven is great, and it's so nice, it's free, like a bird." or Charlie an old teacher who is able to spend the bulk of the time in the Alaskan wilds playing with bears. He doesn't care about whether people think he is a good person. He will do what's right for him, and does what is in his heart. A father who, in spite of his condition of heart, listened in response to his son's request to take on Ironman with him. The father packed, pulled and carried his son around the race because he spent the rest of his life on wheelchair and could not take on the challenge by himself. In fact, Brett Favre, who retired as the NFL's top-performing offensive lineman, and who is now willing to admit that he wasn't enough, was not sufficient. In a bid to confront the media and the team he played for and teammates, he's committed to achieving his goals.

We should all not become extreme skiers in their lives and develop. In fact it would be a disservice to the Mother Earth in the event that we did this. What number of avalanches could one woman endure? The key is to slow in order to make the most profound of our dreams can are realized and used as a way to boost our everyday performance in the things we do. Little steps that could be made will provide the base for staying in the midst of sleep. Learn to be confident enough to ask anyone for help. Go throughout the day saying good-bye to all you encounter and expressing your anger in opposition to injustice, doing an attitude, establishing a dialogue with someone you don't know, speak to a person who is pursuing the dream job, or in order to find out all you can about subjects that you are interested in. Each little action gives us fresh knowledge and illumination, and allows us to grow better.

The act of not having my ego pressure upon me is a worry for me. the way I am perceived in the future, and also how I was able to interact with my adventurous child, and how I lived my everyday life. The more I realized how much more look at myself as different than other people as I grow older, the more I realize who I am. I'm more who I is, and this lets me be my true self and be curious about and to ask the questions I was able to ask when I was a kid.

Each step you take will give the confidence you need to go ahead. Your work is enjoyable and will fill you. Soon you'll be at the edge that you endured for so long in order to stay clear of.

Take Action

Who, what, when, where what, how, when, and how to effectively act.

There are four actions to communicate your imagination and the ability to feel, see and create a physical thing:

1. Choose what you would like to achieve

2. Believe it's now.

3. Be open and willing to receive suggestions

4. Get involved

When you're involved in the three initial steps elements, every resource required to achieve what you're looking for is moving towards you. However, it's through your actions that you make it tangible appearance. With no effort, the physical process isn't it? Your "desire" is just another "delicious idea".

"Fear" is usually the motive behind our inaction. This could be fear of being rejected fears of making mistakes, criticism, changes, fears of being a failure (the list of fears that could be feared is lengthy) and even old stories. Instead of dwelling on what is the "why" of not acting rather, we will look at the five things that are essential to taking decision-making.

Who? You are the one. There is no one else who can do anything to improve the way you feel, except for you! Anything less than that is an act of sacrifice. Look out for situations which "look like" so that they are the fault of someone else. I've struggled with this over the years! It's painful to admit it, but the truth. Who is the one who does it? We all have an idea.

why? It allows you to be able to receive the things you desire. No action, no reception. Consider it like this: that you're in an unlit home. No light can enter. It is cold, lonely and depressed in darkness. The sun shines. The sun shines on the home. This is now available However, you need to get involved and then open the latch on your receiver. How do you earn Winning?

How do you determine your physique. Get moving! Call the number, call the number, and then say If that's the phone you're calling. You're thinking whether Gloria isn't calling you! What can you do to make it physically?

when? Now, it is the sole time that to take action. It's been a while since the past has passed and can't be addressed the future of it cannot be predicted. It is possible to be afraid. Do what you can to take action. If you do then, you're done right now.

Where? Are you acting on the issues you face now? The things you can't do if you'd like to accomplish. Consider the possibility. What would happen to your life when you closed your eyes inside that cold, dark home? What is your operating location you have been?

Do not move forward in your fear of change

What can make a man a woman of adulthood fearful of the summer months? Fear of heights, the fear of being lonely and the fear of dark as well as the fear of snakes, fear of moving into a new city, the fear being unsuccessful, the fear of failure, and the fear of seeing a dentist the doctor. Doctors are the most common. When I was a kid and my mom told me that I was likely to drown if didn't wait for one hour before going to the pool. I was led to believe that, if I took a trip to the ocean or a pool following dinner, I'd fall into the depths. If we are afflicted with superstitious fears or genuine fears, it's an aspect of our human experience. Problems arise when fears limit our development, hinder our ability to make changes, and restrict our choices when it comes to life.

The psychoanalysis pioneer, Sigmund Freud, hypothesised that at the age of six we had already been traumatized by the values and behavior of our family. The fear of losing our family or separation, rejection feeling empty and insecure are normal worries that can sabotage the innocence that we had in our early years and carry on into adulthood when they don't express themselves and are not healed.

Children are innate and soak up everything around them like sponges. As early as they are educators and parents encourage us to recall our worst memories. Fear is integrated in the "subconscious" and build a defense that helps us stay stout or firmly defended against threat. Children experience feelings of anxiety, tears and shyness prior to being able to communicate. Children are often disciplined by parents and do not ask them to think about their feelings and the reasons behind them. This can stifle our natural desire to change and grow.

As an example, at age eight my daughter Lara would wake up each at night, dreaming about the death of her family and world destruction. If her father and I let her feel and share these thoughts We help her explore her internal resources in order to discover the absurdity of life and the necessity to love, and the dread of losing it.

Anne Schafer, a therapist who is also the creator of When Society Becomes Addictive, Escape from Intimacy and other books about addiction and recovery stated, "We are increasingly aware of corruption, collapse financial and fear that pornography networks are taking away our children. " nuclear war is the real threat of food shortages and conflict all over the world. The market for antidepressants is never better. Depression and apathy have been equated with a need to adapt. Instead of searching for innovative strategies to adapt instead, we get more comfortable and defensive of what is normal. "According to Schafer, our society creates a system that alleviates fears with drugs, consumerism and the need to be perfect." Schafer stated: "The addiction scares us, we do not touch and we are too busy to challenge the system. "

The majority of us avoid our anxieties and are confined within our own prisons created by us. The emotional impact of change can bring up painful memories that are easier to forget than declare.

But the longer we ignore this emotion, the higher it'll grow. The force of emotion is comparable to the power of a bomb. It can't be contained in a bowl of powder. It'll blast off or explode. When we suppress our fears and anxiety, it could turn into despair or anger. Such a behavior can make us feel old and in a position to accept and be part of the world. If we wish to make a change then we need to be able to be able to express ourselves, feel as well as acquire.

Engage deeply and strive to achieve visions or hopes to face our biggest anxieties and break away from our rigid and comfortable areas. If we don't, we'll keep playing the blame game based on the past as a excuse to not change. How much do we say we want? In what extent are you accountable for your personal good?

MaryAnn is 38 and is married for six years. MaryAnn says that she "loves" her husband but she isn't "in love" with him. She is ready to let him go however she is unable to give up. Do not engage in intimate conversations with your husband because you do more than you should. He is always there because he's afraid to avoid privacy or be confronted by the abuses of his children.

John 53 year old John conceals his distaste for his wife. The cost of the family is higher even though she'd like to get retired, she's not able due to the amount of debt she's taken on. He worries that a woman might judge him as weak if the truth is revealed.

In the event that MaryAnn and John let their fears hinder their desire to transformation, they'll lose their motivation and plunge into stagnation. Growth means to be able to enjoy the inalienable right of life, and to the liberty of expressing our wishes, dreams and fears.

The process of change involves many phases

You can start from where you're at. We all have our faults.

Review the pattern of repetition and ideas that trigger thoughts that make you feel restricted.

Be kind and loving. Avoid making judgments. The use of comparison, criticism, and critique are likely to cause fear and resistance. The change is not ours to make.

The things you pay attention to are going to draw you in. Focus on the things you already own and not the things you don't have. Take time to be grateful.

Changes will cause tears, anger and sadness. Don't blame yourself. Make sure you take care of yourself.

Begin a journal, meditate on, draw, or play with it and stroll in a tranquil way. The instructions come from within silence.

Be confident in the process. Be confident.

Don't be fooled by those that say that you can't accomplish it.

Take small steps. If you don't think you're required to write an entire book, write one sentence each day. Do something that you enjoy and it will do the same to your benefit.

Discover ways you can feel secure in darkness. What can you do regardless of your fear?

Don't give up and don't ever let up!

It is about self-acceptance, healing, and the ability to make a. Be aware of your anxieties, and focus on what inspires you and take action!

Chapter 2: What Is The Motivation Behind People's Actions?

The test was to make you navigate your vehicle between cones, without touching them. Simple enough, surely? Let's take a look at what it can do for you.

Scenario no. 1: You're an experienced motor.

As a result that driving between them is simple.

Scenario no. 2. You've not climbed before.Result You'll doubt the first time. Perhaps I can try it at all since there's nothing to lose.

Scenario no. 3. You've previously never attempted to climb before. However, this time the grayness disappears and people go by to observe what transpires. You now have eyes on your head, and you're listening to their conversations about each other. I don't think I'm capable, the crash is inevitable and it's foolish to attempt to do it, etc.

Therefore it is likely that you won't attempt to do anything out of fear of appearing embarrassed or losing your face.

Scenario no. 4: Similar to scenario 3. This time, however, I'm sporting a gun over my skull and amthreatening that I'll shoot you if don't attempt.

So, you'll likely!

Scenario no. 5: The same scenario as 3. However, this time there's no weapon and people are just snatching at your. They are encouraging you, and convince you to: Give, shoot and there's nothing to lose, leave to the next location, etc.

So, you'll likely!

Scenario no. 6: Similar to scenario 3. You are discouraged. Yet, I placed an enviable million dollars worth of money near the bottom of an Arrow. The choice is yours to try.

So, you'll most likely!

This time, I'd like you to pay attention to one of the stages. 1, 4, 5 and 6. The four possibilities are that you've gotten yourself the chance. How do you feel about it? Answering this problem is the question of what motivates people to act, and why do not. It is the reason why a small percentage of people take on a task or face a problem; whether in sports and business venture or in everyday life and why some do are not. Two important points should be made at this point.

A) in a) in. 1 acted since it was the entire results. There was no doubt in the possibility that you might not succeed. You trusted yourself. What is important is "TERMINATION of the desired result".

What did you do to gain the sense of security? Your driving experience. It is important to remember Experience leads to security

B) in the n. 4., was taken action even if there was no result. Because? Your environment has been stimulating. This has helped you increase your efforts, improve your endurance, and to push yourself. Since your website has taken responsibility for your accomplishments.

You should remember that the environmental conditions dictate your behavior.

In the case of c) in the n. 5. done something in the being afraid of loss of your life. In fact it was the fear loss MORE than the loss of a life. There was more at stake If you chose not to make an effort to do anything.

The fact that your worry of losing something other than the color of the contest will dictate your choices.

D) in the n. 6, you did what you did as a reward because it was enticing. In reality, if were not in need of the money, and you're an oaf, your decision would have no reason to take action. If you were a average person, you'd be tempted by a million dollars.

Considerations to make Things to consider: Benefits from personal experience affect your decisions

Three things are what make people behave at an essential level

A) Experience B) Be afraid of loss C) A) Desire to gain personal benefits.

What you decide to do to motivate other people is based on your character and the way you live your living. I'm looking for.

What can you do to ward off fear?

If that were it the case, we might think that these authorised entities are not able to control other people, and I am not sure it would result in an advantage for the people seeking to control the world, and get the best results in the future. While it might appear like a conspiracy it is important to remember that we all are in the habit of spreading the fear through the interactions we have with other people as well as the "knowledge" we pass on. Take a look at what he says or does, and you could be shocked by the evidence that shows he's been taken captive and promoted the things is he hoping to gain. That's how amazing the genius of the whole thing, and which we all take part in without realizing that we are part of it.

Thus, I feel that the majority of anxieties aren't natural, and especially when it comes to anxiety that blocks people from trying out new ideas and forces us to stick with the more secure path with which we feel comfortable. Easy. The fear has affected every one of us, and have been passed through generations (we are currently gaining enormous speed with modern methods which can accelerate the process significantly) and allowing for a type self-sufficient population which doesn't require direct control. Fear is the primary reason that everything stays online. prevents the emergence of radical and critical ideas that could be a threat to the state and creates an uncompromising population that seeks tranquility and security from the governing authority. As we slowly get off the beaten path There will always be an event of significance that puts everyone to sleep the way a clock does. This mechanism works perfectly.

Have a look around, you likely haven't thought much about your feelings in a particular moment however, consider if you can identify any of these patterns that appear familiar to you. Do I do what is expected of me? Do I have a genuine job? My family and friends respect my work enough? It could be that I need to earn more as well as more items to gain greater respect. Perhaps I'll need to take longer hours to earn higher wages, more work as well as more respect. Perhaps I shouldn't forget my family and friends as I am using all my time looking for work, money and connections. Son of #! "$%@ I'm exhausted by all this, yet I don't have the time to rest because sleep is my most needed thing. I'm sure it's an extremely stressful time in my life. It's likely to get better in the near future. It's been awhile before I've thought about that what's the date for when the future is going to be here? Ah, damn, life stinks! Am I too negative?

It's not that difficult and is an enormous waste of time! However, it's an illness that is affecting everyone. At the root of all this devastation, naturally it is the worry. Most likely, you've spent a good deal of time either consciously or not, dispersing the entirety of your issues (we are believers in the concept that there are "problems" even if there are no evidence to support the nature of them) as a collective of tiny and large and oversized small that all boils down to the fact that you are afraid, pure and immediately. . The understanding, even though it could sound negative, can be very positive since you begin to get your eyes open and when you are awake it is the last time you'll get to rest ever again. If you are feeling guilty about the slowdown you experienced, it's not really your blame in the first instance (it's your own fault if opt to deny the reality and remain in a state of fear) And the third wrong choice will send you on exactly the same direction as you are afraid! !

Fear for the reason that it works for people who are more educated than you are and who feel it is their duty to manage your fears. So, the government, parents or religions, and even us make use of fear in order to influence. That's how we were instructed and conditioned to do your work, or else you'll never get into fifth grade. If you do, you won't find a job. You could end up as sponsored, and no one would like it. Fear not, but better not play because I'm gonna ruin my life. Thank you for all the great advice and I did not realize the importance of it to me. Anything good you share with me I share it with other people for certain. This is how the cycle starts! ...

Now it is possible that he's contemplating, ok but what if it's not that much of a change in this area, that's what the world does that's why we have to take it in stride. There is a certain sense in accepting the world as it is since at the end of the day there is no place other than here and now regardless of how we get there. So, accepting reality is an important step and any resistance to the way things are, can only be described as a kind of foolishness. How could we possibly expect the world to adhere to our narrow notion of what we want it to be? Millions of people, with billions of definitions, how can all the world's dimensions be accommodated simultaneously? It's impossible, and boring with regard to this. Therefore, yes I'm in agreement, and accept that, but don't give up on your search for consciousness, since the more aware, the less you fear.

Be aware that we're not attempting to eradicate the fear of being afraid because it's a normal part of the human condition and our sole aim is to allow fear to control our lives because fear is the sole "sin" (if I can utilize a term that is misunderstood by many for the fact that) that exists. Each unpleasant thing you imagine is rooted in the fear of being deceived (fear of truth) and theft (fear of being lost) or cheating (fear of being hurt) or any other such thing. While we try to stop people from performing these crimes however, are we scared of the consequences from the practice of the religion (fear of God) and the justice system (fear of prison)? Ironically, when we aren't able to make people afraid, then we do never have to worry about the first time! It's a good idea to take a step back and look at what we're doing and accept who we are. Through this recognition and acceptance, we've brought up some issues and have moved forward on a direction that, I believe, can make you feel more at ease than living with anxiety.

The second part is hardest to master, and it's challenging for many people to jump into the new mindset and then revert back to the way they have been, and I've been there frequently. The question you should think about in nearly all situations is whether you're scared or simply because it's healthy for you. If you begin to think that is the way to think, you'll be amazed by how much you can handle. Consider the fear of dying as an example. If you've been brought up in the context of many Western religious beliefs, then there's likely to be a lot of fear and confusion concerning this idea. If we were to think of ourselves as brave, there's an occasional ache concerning the notion of the unknowable and death and the unknown. This is, of course common, though I typically apply the phrase with a little slack. True, it's a reasonable feeling because you were taught from the age of a child to be scared of the possibility of death.

But, it isn't normal in that we've taken on the most natural thing and it is almost as if born in the right place and created something that is considered unnatural and should be avoided at all cost. Actually, what could be the purpose of living in the absence of dying? It is impossible to comprehend the way life is portrayed when we don't have anything to measure. Furthermore, no person that is truly minded wants to live for ever regardless of whether we believe that it's a good idea at times. This would be a miserable existence and will likely need us to end. However, due to some reason it is our nature to seek out something that has absolutely no sense. We humans always think the idea that "grass, on the other hand, is greener" We know it is more likely than the alternatives would be a lot more appealing. If we had greater "control", this will appear better.

But, the truth is that the reason that life is able to be enjoyable is that there exists the "calendar" that motivates us to explore new ideas. If we don't have this notion of time, it'd be absurd to try things to get the chance opportunities. It is also a fact that we do not remember to end up dying more or less each the night before bedtime. We don't know about the world around us, struggle to recall our past and cannot connect effectively in a meaningful way with "the living" while we are asleep. The truth is that we have been "dead" during this period prior to "birth", but this time in our lives is not one of the issues. Through the years it has become clear that our current self is different from the self of just a couple of years earlier (all the cells of our body differ and our brains are different as well, yet we do our best to make sure that some aspects of ourselves from doing too excessively to make others feel confused). Our ego is an important aspect in our discontent. It is a consuming obsession for the person I think of as me, to the extent that the entirety of our lives revolves around the defense of the "me" at all costs. However, of nature appears to be a breeze without no drama or pity on self.

Imagine how different our lives would be if everyone considered death to be as a kind of illusion which helps the remainder of our dreams to be more logical. There shouldn't be a lot of in the way of death's mystery and this would render it an unsettling and frightening experience. Another perspective is that, if your life could be described as a dream birth would result in you falling asleep and then falling asleep, only to awake! It is evident that there are a variety of methods to see the larger picture. However, there is a reason why the majority people choose to stick with the depressing and boring perspective that provides the impression of imminent death at the base of our heads. We think we're qualified and have a grasp of enough about the universe that we can draw this conclusion. Crazy and arrogant!

The time is now to question who actually has anything to gain from being misinformed. We mentioned, everybody is scared of losing their lives and wants to guard themselves. Another logical option is to utilize the fear of losing to exploit the weaknesses of others and gain your own goals to make improvements. Thus, TV, which is which is used to communicate all the worries which we face today, tells that we should be worried about terror, war and not having enough stuff and not being a good friend to others and so on. We are forced to surrender our civil rights as well as to choose certain people as government officials, and to join companies (to increase the wealth of societies) for the purpose of earning cash to purchase products, make payments to tax payers, and a myriad of other things are probably not even known to us. Keep in mind that all is an exercise and fear is merely a word which is not logical in the context of analysis.

The only method by which the fear of losing can be used as a strategy is if everyone believes that there's something in the balance and a stake to be taken. It is common for us to get caught up by the game just like the other players around us. we recall how crucial the game is, and we also recognize each other even however the reality is that there's no reason to be afraid (everyone can be thankful to wake out of bed and then when you wake up to nightmares, you realize there's nothing to worry about It was all an illusion). We tend to ourselves and the people we love until we realise that all can't be achieved. That doesn't mean it is impossible to live our lives the way you want it to be, however, we require the knowledge to recognize that we will have to go through various situations that we are unable to avoid or should not be avoiding (like dying).

It's likely that belief that certain things were outside of our control ought to give us a sense of calm (since this takes the burden off the shoulders of our backs). Yet, we chose to take control of all things, even though it was futile. There's no doubt there's plenty of untruths about this but here we are yet again. Until the world wakes up to the reality of this, we'll remain in this area of change until it is made better. It is likely that you aren't able to see the solution to this since we're all immersed in our daily routines. I'm not one of them. The goal here isn't to suddenly get rid of all fear in order to jump ahead and instantly alter your perception of the world.

Make a promise to never alter the way you watch a television or a family person tries to scare you with things that you believe you ought to be terrified about (remember that they make this decision because they are terrified). Being able to teach other people the techniques we employ to keep our heads on straight is the first essential stage to become the self-sufficient and powerful individuals which we must be. As more people understand that the reason why they're scared is the fact that it will benefit somebody else The more people get up and realize there's no reason to be concerned. It's just how she is.

The time is now to get involved

This action is often referred to as a substance that guarantees the results. There is no work, and there's no result. It's that simple! A lot of people talk and plan about what they'd like to achieve, however when it comes down to actually doing some thing, they never take action!

Over the years, it's been said "Faith without works has no end useful" It's an actual truth! The power of affirmations is not enough. Positive thoughts and affirmations will only help only if you do something. It's not a good idea to say that you'll be successful while inactive. It is a lie, and nothing happens. You are not simply the "connoisseur" of things or an exuberant person, but being a performer.

This is an action that will ensure your success not your thoughts. The plan will fail when you stop taking doing it. The actions you take speak louder than what you say. There are people who doubt the things you have to say however, they'll believe the actions you take since they see.

Keep in mind that inactivity causes anxiety. It builds confidence. If you're looking to get over anxiety, don't stay at home, and you're thinking about the issue. Get out and get to work!

This is the main message I want to convey If you want to achieve it in your lifetime Begin!

Get started today.

The time has come to begin writing this novel.

The time is now to begin this venture

This is the time to announce the product or service you've been waiting for.

This is the time to invite this wonderful person for a chat

Now is the time to finish reading that book you've been wanting to go through

You're ready to pick up your mobile and call without fear to this stressed customer

You're ready to grab the phone to talk with whomever you'd like to speak to.

Don't wait any longer, no more delays, and more the need to reprogramme. The time is now to get active.

Do something Take action, and you'll be amazed at the ease it can be to get something done regardless of the challenges you might meet in the pursuit of your desired outcome. You shouldn't simply plan and contemplate something. Think about take act. Make it happen! The older men have said to me "It's not what you know; it's what you do with what you know."

Chapter 3: Self-Criticism

It's great that you do the best you can and be as normal as you can be. It's logical to examine your poor outcomes in your life and strive to make improvements the in the future. However, it's very easy to be overly self-critical. Self-criticality that is excessive will hinder one's progress as well as good mental well-being. A high level of self-criticism can harm confidence in yourself and self-esteem.

Think about these warning signs that indicate you could be being too self-critical of yourself.

You're paralyzed. One sign that you're extremely dangerous to your own is the absence of taking action. If you've been within the same circumstance for long periods of duration, then you're far too risky for yourself. If you were not, you'd take action and create positive change within your own life.

It is difficult to forgive other people. If you can't forgive yourself, then you can't accept forgiveness from others. If you are able to accept forgiveness and let yourself go and others, it is possible to do so for other people that you meet.

There is no way to be content with the results you have achieved. You don't care about reducing 10 minutes from the time he has set of 10 kilometers or getting an medical certificate. It is a source of frustration for you due to the fact that you didn't not place in the top 10 or go to the medical school of Harvard.

There is no insurance coverage for you. You need to feel comfortable enough with your self-confidence. Being assertive also comes with the fear of being rejected. Self-criticization can raise the anxiety over being rejected from others.

Everyone says negative things. It is true that a small proportion of your internal dialogs is not much of an issue. But, the continuous stream of self-criticism can be extremely damaging. Imagine that your child realizes it's impossible to achieve anything and has to quit making an effort. This may seem absurd from this perspective.

Your chronicles are inefficient. A poor performance can be an indication and motive to self-criticism. Low performance on a regular basis can be a signal to take act!

Some people are comfortable to criticize your actions. Most people do not like to criticise others. But, if they hear how they constantly criticize your actions, they're likely to believe that they could take part with the criticism.

It is normal to criticize yourself on a regular basis in general, not only on specific instances. It is different telling yourself you're not the best tennis player and telling yourself that you're bad in all areas of your life. This generalization is untrue and extremely destructive.

A failure in one particular area is not a sign of the victim. It's not rational.

It's your opinion. Even though you've every right to not tell your neighbor that you look overweight in your outfit You should feel comfortable telling them the title of the book you love. If you're uncomfortable speaking your mind and you are concerned whether other people might judge the way you dress or even say something that is wrong.

It is easy to spend too much time thinking about your errors. Do you have the ability to take action quickly following an instant of reflection, or do you criticise your errors for a longer time?

There is no need to seek help. Helping yourself should not be a problem. More support you receive, the more you can benefit! Do you worry about deeming that you're inadequate? If so it's because you're not being enough critical of your self.

There is no way to give a single positive review. Everyone has something they excel at. Maybe you realize you excel in a few areas, yet you don't think you are worthy of recognition. Whatever the case, you're self-critical.

Your self-esteem is weakened by performing overly self-critical thoughts. It also affects your performance and mental health. Be aware of how badly you've caused yourself to be a victim of self-criticism. Take your lessons learned and then apply your knowledge in a positive way.

Negatively criticize yourself with humor and laughter.

Everybody suffers from self-criticism at times. It can be helpful. There are many valuable opinions from people who have critics. Self-criticism, however, can turn into unwholesome and trigger thoughts of no significance. It's helpful to counter this tendency. Humor is an easy and effective method of doing it. Through educating yourself and gaining the perspective you need!

Make an effort to smile at your inner critic by using the following suggestions:

Strange audio recordings

There are times when we fall into the practice of telling a tragic tale about ourselves "Why do this keep happening to me? What makes my the life of a solitary person so hard? ..." What would happen when you hear this tale using a humorous soundtrack? You can listen to the exact story but with a circus soundtrack playing in the background, or knowing that you can tell it's a Benny Hill song!

The clown in you

Pay attention to what the person are telling yourself by being critical. Examine the manner in which he speaks to you. Imagine the clown right in front of you. take a look at his huge colorful shoes. Check out the crazy colors of his outfit. Apply a funky makeup to your face and give it a huge smile. What sort of amusing hat do you think of? Recently, I've listened to clowns criticize each other the hat, however with a humorous voice.

Magic is the word that describes it.

Do you critique yourself? For instance) "I'm such an idiot!"

What happens when you transform one of your keywords into something inanimate, such as"paper cup" "paper cup"?

"I'm a paper cup!"

Enjoy trying out other things. Through laughter, you can forget all the negative associations that are within your brain.

Micky mouse

How do you sound in a situation where you are criticizing? Does it sound like a soft voice?

You can listen to the same words that he is saying, only with the sound that of Mickey Mouse. How is the tone that comes from Daffy Ducks and Sylvester Cat?

Fun and most enjoyable!

Do you recall having a conversation about one of your experiences with your friend who believed that it was among the most hilarious things they've seen or heard? Both laughed!

When you think of your good memories of laughter take a moment to think about the recently self-doubts. Reconnect with your pal in remembrance of laughter. You can then return to your self-critical thoughts, and also laugh!

Humour and laughter is among the fastest methods to deal with extreme severity. Utilizing simple strategies such as the ones below, you will be able to master your own self-criticism, and also gain significant internal creativity.

You must be creative and critical.

Critical thinking can improve the quality of our work and creativity to achieve excellence. If the criticism is based on excessive obsessiveness or an unrealistic view of self critique can be harmful and limited, which can compromise our creativity and safety.

Some creative individuals who have been recognized for their talent they may experience negative thinking and fears.

Before receiving the Booker Prize, the Irish author John Banville considered the most famous prize for novel writing and was convinced that his chances of winning would be slim; "I am inclined to think that all my books are bad," the writer declared.

A lot of talented actors claim that they don't watch films. In the case of close-ups on movie screens 20 feet tall it is difficult to not criticize their looks or performance. Joaquin Phoenix said he did not approve of the way he sported his lips or teeth. Kate Winslet admitted that before going to the movies she often thought: "I'm a cheater, and I get fired ... I'm fat, and I'm ugly."

According to research on talent the most creative and gifted individuals often face excessive perfectionists, as well as unreasonable standards that could cause an excessive amount of critique.

Lesley Sword, director of the creative and gift service in Australia She says children who are gifted are "very active and critical when they judge others. They display their frustration with their own lives and imagine what they could be. ."... They are obsessed with perfectionism, against which they evaluate their own performance and may feel dejected or even depress themselves because of the perception of their failure. "

The children who have strong talents can be applauded for their imaginative ideas, but they don't learn that criticizing can help or that it can take patience and time to develop the talents they have. When they are adults, if the image either in their work, book or film doesn't meet the standards fast sufficient or "perfectly", they can become very critical of their work.

Men's norms are generally based on to recognize a "good" creative work, that are based on masculine values and the arts, as opposed to acknowledging women as equal, though possibly different, with respect to aesthetic sensibility.

The personal feelings of the owner may also lead to self-reflection. Jonathan Safran Foer "I can be very hard on myself, I convince myself to deceive people, or I am convinced that people love books for the wrong reasons."

Identity concepts can limit your ideas of identity. The director Jane Campion, hired for "Piano" and other films has said "I never had the confidence to make a film, I just thought it was a genius, and it was apparent to me that he was not one of them. "

The Nobel laureate of poetry and writing Czeslaw Milosz had already stated: "From the first writing, it is a way to overcome my real or imaginary uselessness".

Based on the research they found that these are not uncommon instances. People with extraordinary abilities are confronted with difficult emotions, such as feelings of inadequacy or inferiority, as well as critical self-assessment.

Mary-Elaine Jacobsen, in her book Gifted Adults, talks about common judgments people receive, as well as derogatory remarks which can be interpreted in the long run as self-criticism "Why not slow down? "; "You worry about everything!"

"You cannot keep a thing? ": "You are too emotional and emotional! "; "You have to take things the hard way!"

A way to combat critics, even you, is to appear amusing. In the comedy television show "Bones", FBI's talkative agent Seeley Booth (played by David Boreanaz) often comments on the forensic anthropologist, Dr. Always and her squinting. "

She then responds "You mean brilliant people and basic reasoning skills?" In the following scene she seems to be frustrated about her self-esteem. "You're so smart," and she responds, "Yes, I'm smart, but it has nothing to do with my buttocks."

It is a form of the approach used in cognitive-behavioural therapy to help people overcome depression, anxiety and other problems: become aware of negative and self-critical thoughts, examine them carefully and logically, then modify or reformulate them.

They are usually absurd beliefs about life can be or ought to "be" and can become simple responses to stressors that are too general to be pinpointed.

As an example, you could be thinking, "I am too sensitive." What does that mean? Are you too sensitive to something? Certain circumstances can create more pain than you'd like to endure. Amy Brenneman (the star of the film "Rating Amy"] once stated, "I am too sensitive to be able to see most reality shows, which is very painful for me."

It is, however, a more precise and exact assertion, which is why it's true, that I'm "too sensitive". Being sensitive, in the end, is an asset for anyone.

Many people are able to find well-crafted statements which can be frequently read to combat critiques and unreliable and limited thoughts.

Another way to regulate self-critical comments is to inquire whether, if you were to make comments to a close friend or a child, could you be able to help them? Are you able to encourage and help those around you?

Some critical thinking can be positive, provided they're not excessive, obsessive, or fanciful. For instance, as Will Smith pointed out, "I keep going because I doubt myself, it makes me feel better ... It sets me apart."

Change self-criticism to self-pity!

Are you of the opinion that in order for you to be successful, you need be relentless with your self? Do you think compassion is an insecurity and a great strategy to minimize your own self-esteem? Would you like to change your perspective if you realize the self-pity you feel can improve the quality of your life and increase your capacity to deal with the challenges of your life?

Research has shown that self-esteem is a strong correlate with wellbeing. Self-pity is more than being self-critical or abrasive to yourself. Self-pity is the act of treating yourself with respect, compassion and affection by providing warmth and non-judgment rather than lowering self-criticism. Like self-esteem and confidence, self-esteem does not come from feeling happier when you are with other people. In fact, compassion relies upon accepting all aspects of their individual capabilities as well as limitations.

Self-criticism is an integral part of existence for a lot of people. It's commonplace to be in a highly competitive world to be looking for weaknesses as well as the shortcomings of other people and even ourselves. Self-critical thinking tends to are a result of an inner dialogue, continuous (and sometimes violent) statements, as well as gratitude for the things is happening. The self-criticism that we engage in can lead us to an attitude which is shattered, unhappy and anxious.

The most effective method to defeat self-criticism is by understanding and accept it. Be aware of your self-criticism and try to defend yourself and manage your actions. Though you may believe that you should use self-criticism as a way to get yourself motivated studies have shown that those who have compassion are equally likely to have higher standards and follow through with them as people who are not compassionate. You can offer protection more efficiently through letting go of your judgement and allowing yourself to be compassionate and acceptance of your actual human experience.

Self-esteem improves your capacity to change and be more comfortable in the presence of personal limitations or extreme living circumstances. When a person is stressed, they are unhappy with himself and creates physical and mental tension and weakens the capacity to deal with stress. Through showing compassion, you will be able to reduce anxiety, boost the self-confidence of your friends and family members, as well as increase your energy and satisfaction. The research has proven that people that are strong and confident tend to create certain plans to accomplish their objectives and live an enviable lifestyle.

For a greater happy, healthier and more enjoyable life, don't judge your self! Be the same person with the same respect and love that you show to your friend, or even to a stranger. Genuine sympathy is not dependent on what you believe in or the virtues.

I am sorry for you!

Chapter 4: Self-Critical Thinking Is The Basis Of Many Emotional Problems.

This is all you have do to make yourself emotionalally sick. It's a real emotional reaction to something, accompanied by a delicious and satisfying self-critical exercise under challenging circumstances.

The thing is, it's not simply a game of the words. The viewpoint: it is the view of self-confidence. It's an instant picture that you give to the person you are. When you speak this, since you're at the center of an emotional moment, and our minds retain the information more effectively when we express them when we are in an emotional high Your story will convey confidence through your body and brain.

As this feeling is emotionally intense, the unconscious brain believes it's real since it "feels it" and suddenly sees the movement as an issue. It's not the kind of scenario where you are experiencing the intense emotion it is, but oh you are not. It's you, O my God in error!

It reacts emotionally to its perceived "internal problem" by producing another emotional response to block the first reaction. an attack that is double-sided. The feeling of guilt is felt, as you're embarrassed to feel uneasy and uncomfortable.

After that, as the initial emotion is not ready to go away, and another response is also wanting to leave, you create further responses to maintain your primary and secondary responses on the same page, which increases. Each time you answer another question you continue to tell yourself that you are more insane than you really are. Now you are at war with your self. An all-out, doomed, and doomed conflict erupted within the vicinity.

Three seconds. The words which generated the medium conceal the intensity of emotion generated. The brain of his mind has been manipulated numerous times. It has obliterated his mind as well as his memory to the extent that he doesn't know the actions he took in order to cause this preposterous problem.

You've spent weeks or months trying to understand your emotional response by observing your point perspective, but you're unclear of what's wrong you. You think you know the answer.

Thoughts often pop up in the middle of nowhere and don't expect to see them. However, when they do pop out of the blue, we may think that we should have discovered them earlier (by by the way, don't do this for self-pity) to not have found previously conceived ideas, because that's what thoughts do.

It's the idea of an "inside view". What will you notice when you look at this concept? The self-critical phrases you considered for a long time: "I'm crazy." You will witness: the thoughts of judgment which caused him to develop an immediate and self-critical view that shattered the thought of him and his belief but without suspicion at the time.

Within the same time it is possible to rescind this view. Be aware of how effective the initial three seconds were, and what you can do to ensure that you don't repeat the mistake.

If you experience emotions and you notice you're likely to be criticising your self and you'll have to be stopped (please).

Self-criticism when you are in the midst of an emotional conflict Don't do it.

You discover that your husband has had an affair with your sibling, the two of your relations at once. And you are compelled to confront the two of them instead of imagining "crazy" and starting to fight. Find the solution to find the practical and expert help you need to extract your emotions in a safe manner from your body and avoid any self-doubt, injury or self-injury.

Do not permit abusers or those who don't consider you a person to imposition their ideas on your mental space. They should not give you criticism of yourself, and then to take it in and then apply the impression as if they were self-centered or untruths. It can be devastating.

Many emotional disorders result from a basic belief that the self-criticism "I should not feel it" and then an assumption that just since you experience what your feelings, you can not have the ability to get rid of it.

Be aware of how you feel. Accept it regardless of the intensity Find a positive solution to get it out of your body. Your odds of remaining more emotionally healthy are greater. Take note of the circumstances that have triggered the feelings you are experiencing, since this could mean you must take any form of action to get rid of the feeling.

Every aspect the way I've helped someone with an emotional issue (including myself) I have heard that the very concept of criticism is collapsing:

"The fool; the dangerously dumb, fragile and sensitive (you weren't sensitive enough) Incompetent, it's only me and I'll not change. I've never been a good person in situations such as this (no this is not a logical response, and it's not mistaken to be identifying with it). '

The best ideas are to be discovered. Locate them.

Are you familiar with the three second time limit? Avoid that. Get up. Allow yourself to become a fully complete human being. It can be emotional and intense. There have been for a long time that we've felt (and definitely releasing our emotions in the course of time, and returning to the joy of life).

Tips for Overcoming Negative Self-Criticism

Self-esteem sufferers tend to view themselves as negative. The following section provides the reasons why self-criticizing yourself cannot be true.

What is the reason negative self-criticism is not valid?

Everyone has many factors that define who they truly are. These aspects are all able to be evaluated. But, trials is conducted only by prejudgment, which makes it an opinion that is subjective. This is merely the impression of the trial, and not the final truth.

A person's character is a mix of many traits, it is impossible to conclusively criticise only one characteristic.

* Human beings are human and can have a virtually unlimited variety of attributes.

* The properties aren't permanent, they're in constant changing. It is often the situation that determines them.

It's difficult to compare things because they can't be accurately assessed.

Because people consist of many factors, it's impossible to evaluate the whole person. Only you can determine that the character or behavior of a person are specific. Individuals with low self-esteem form drastic judgments of their own self-esteem. This can trigger feelings of superiority or inadequacy, which is an incorrect method of thinking.

When they stop from making extreme negative judgements those lacking self-esteem can find an increase in happiness and peace of mind living. If they continue to do so certain psychological issues could develop. These include:

1.) APD The person gets shattered by criticism and is unable to make decisions, and becomes dependent upon other people.

2.) Beware of Personality Disorders The person is unable to do actions that could result in the possibility of being subject to criticism.

3.) The paranoid personality disorder The person in question does not trust others anymore and expects bad reviews and is prone to reading innocent remarks.

4.) Schizoid: A person is unable to express their thoughts and feelings, but is indifferent to relationships with others.

5.) Schizotypal Personality Disorder: The person is suffering from depersonalization and false perceptions.

Eliminate self-criticism, boost enthusiasm and be happy.

The ability to make time for every minute is at the core of the heartbreaking issue of time management. It is amazing to be able to take advantage of the possibilities that life offers it, experiences, and appreciates while we're in the present, completely open to our vitality and our hearts, as well as our imagination and creativity!

Imagine how you'd experience a distinct feeling the self-critical thoughts take away your faith. This is what I'm speaking about. This irritates and degrades your energy levels, which reduces your speed and focus. This is a self-fulfilling prophecy since it's impossible to behave at your best in situations when you behave as your most feared opponent!

It's an area I'd like to emphasize since I'm not just discussing the experience you have of the moment. Life is definitely more interesting when you're active and open. And it's not the same. In fact, the kind of energy you put into a particular moment affects the things you see and what you decide to do as well as what you do next.

The cynical, critical voice we all have is a reflection of the color and energy that is happening and invariably alters the reality like a wave mirror at the carnival. The ability to silence the critical voice and reconnect to your inner self is the equivalent of being able to see again. The world is different now and you are able to embrace the world from its powerful center which transforms every aspect of your life!

What can you do to be able to identify and combat these negative voices? The initial and foremost action is to recognize their existence; we've many of them. The messages they come from are usually ones that were received by him in the early years of his life and were later adapted when his life progressed. These messages are likely to become in such a way that you aren't aware of they exist. It is likely that you constantly transmit messages.

It's an extremely fluid method. It is not just that you talk about the self-criticism you have made throughout your time, but you react. Perhaps you'll reject him with a radical manner, causing you to feel annoyed and defensive. Perhaps you are feeling depressed and even a victim. You can bet that beneath the surface, you are confronted with a range of feelings when you respond to your internal drone critique.

It's a vicious cycle is actually, and it's good to know that you have the ability to intervene and change your behavior anytime that could change the procedure! If he recognizes an internal self-critical thought and compares it with reality and breaks the cycle. If you find that you're depressed because you're responding to your own inner criticism, verify and feel the changes in energy.

Understanding that what your critics say don't reflect the fact and being able to modify and alter their messages can be a powerful device in the heart-based management toolbox.

Consider these issues to regain your energy and happiness and to relive the moments in the best way you can:

What are the most important lessons that have you been absorbing?

What are they saying to you at the bottom of your existence?

What can they do to exhaust you, and even challenge your patience?

What happens if you approach them with compassion and reason?

Be sure to shield your self from criticism.

The internal dialogue, positive or not, is the inner voice. It is the one that speaks to you that aren't spoken in louder voices. How you talk will determine the kind of individual you will become.

The best and worst aspect of the inner dialogue is that you will be able to hear what you are saying. Be honest with yourself and be a victim of your own thoughts. Be gentle with yourself and you'll feel good of your self. Your words can bless you or curse you. it is your sole control over them.

These are the options available to you:

Positive internal conversations are solid, confident and balanced. It's like having a playful, melodious tune that plays within your head to keep you focused on the positive side, look for the positive, or anticipate the best.

Negative internal dialog makes people look unattractive, dumb and uninformed. It's like a continuous sound of complaints, or funeral songs that play within your brain to bring back the horrible things that occurred to you, or may be happening to your.

Which is the most trustworthy voice for you?

Discover how the inner dialog works to your advantage and not for yourself. These are the four ideas that can help you end your negative, negative and repressive self-criticisms that hinder you from:

Take note of yourself. Recall the phrases you use to use to describe yourself. Are you saying things such as "I'm ugly", or "I cannot learn anything new" or "I'm nothing compared to these people" or "I'm not very smart?" I failed mathematics in the seventh class ".

Be aware of what you are saying to yourself. You may be accustomed to self-criticism. This self-criticism may prevent him from being the person God would have wanted him to become.

Your first step towards stopping the internal negative dialogue is to know what you are hearing in your own voice is telling you.

To question you. Self-critical self-belief is most likely incorrect. If you did not do well in math in the seventh grade doesn't suggest that you're foolish. The only thing that matters is you didn't succeed in mathematics in seventh grade.

Request things such as what is the evidence of the information I've just provided? Are you interested in talking to someone else in addition with me? Do you have more constructive and less critical ways of expressing you? There are many ways to convince others to be honest with you aren't you? It is also important to reveal the truth about yourself.

Break into. If you are facing a major issue, your negative voice is saying, "Here we go again, another opportunity to prove how stupid I am!" Refuse to believe it by using positive phrases. You may begin with the words, "It's gone again," but then you need to critique your self. You can stop praying and then say to yourself: "Another opportunity to solve the problem and to be a happy person."

Promise you. It is your sole responsibility to determine your goals and you must promise to be nice towards yourself. Be rid of the self-critical thoughts that make you miserable and replace them by positive and positive messages for yourself.

The negative effects of criticism can be detrimental to success.

Reflection and self-reflection can hinder your ability to be too quick to reach your goals. People always consider others and are concerned much about what others consider us. We strive to please everyone that we come across and appreciate people's views. Problems will increase and expectations won't be realistic at the end of the day, it will be impossible to please everyone. It is not necessary to be concerned about the ones who justify themselves by claiming that they have the right to express their opinions, but they are not worth anything.

We are not thought of according to what we consider. We don't take this into consideration and constantly think about other people's opinions on us. Other people also have opinions about ourselves and how we treat us. It is interesting that both sides overlook this fact.

It is still believed that our issues aren't big enough and that nobody is facing a challenge. It's not an issue but we think that everything around us isn't a issue. It is only our thinking to be a reflection of our difficulties and do not imagine others' practices as our own. We are of the opinion that our issues are our own and our problems can be considered common.

The lack of trust you have will result in you being unnecessarily harsh. People hurt each other, and praise each other. If they continue to do this it will end everyone as a result, and will not succeed in moving forward by putting in the effort and dedication. Even though he doesn't agree with the opinion of another but he still says "yes" because of his insecurity. This may not cause an issue and it may not solve anything.

Our conscience constantly is constantly warning us, and then criticises us with a strong tone. It is a major challenge to us every whenever we are faced with a dilemma or prepare for this job. The awareness is always fast-forward, which puts our preconceived notions to the forefront, as a result of the training by our teachers, parents, and our grandparents. It is believed that our opinions are traditional and standard that will safeguard our rights. However, this isn't the case. Every time we hear them, they warn us of that we've been unable to fulfill our obligations.

If we aren't happy with our own self, then we shouldn't be able to develop a negative impression of yourself. There is no way to satisfy everyone on the planet. Stop these sexy abuses quickly and be more loving to our fellow human beings. Be sure not to judge yourself for every moment and be a victim to an unspoken inner voice warning you of the lack of confidence you have and inadequacy. Certain changes happen with no consent. Be patient and embrace yourself with all your heart in order to build self-esteem.

Develops the ability to become less important

Many of us can love each others with an abundance of love. To love self-love, is a signification of an attainable, perhaps an idealistic idea. But, loving yourself is more complicated and requires you to confront this harsh critic and be able to accept the reality that you are. In the mirror, will you be able to do this with self-acceptance and unconditional respect and love?

The similarities and what you think

Everyone has flaws and discover how to accept one another, and are not ashamed of the fact that they have it. Every person has faults and everyone are, even you, bound by responsibility, so you must take the time to appreciate your uniqueness, your personality and the spirit. If you're gifted and talents, let it shine through when you've got the Achilles heel that annoys you. Wouldn't it be wiser to sing loudly rather instead of muting the voice of one's choice throughout life?

What do you think others will think? Will you remember me angry? If I were you, I'd ask if it was necessary. Surely the most important person you know would be you. Therefore, allow others to criticize them, they have the right to express their opinions and you are entitled to the right to share their thoughts. Look at young children. They play in their own world constantly whirring, screaming or screaming. We can't be satisfied when we cook the mud pie. It is a shame to follow the rules and beliefs of people around you.

If we choose to not follow their wishes and they don't be able to love us any more. It is possible that they feel embarrassed since they're doing something that's not in their normal routine and feel dismayed instead of being able to leave. That is an indication of the quality of your relationship when a minor misunderstanding can stop the relationship. Also, do you have any other issue which you believe could be causing all the influence in your relationship?

How do you feel about it?

It's about placing yourself at the center of your existence. Put your effort into helping your growth. Do what you are able to and acknowledge that you have things you are unable to alter. Make sure you take care of your health, consume healthy food and moderately when the occasion occurs, there's chocolate on the toilet. Although it is essential to stay fit, don't become overwhelmed by your imagination with an unrealistic figure. Accept the body that we are given.

When you're suffering from emotional illness It's very easy to forget about. Try doing something that you enjoy, often at least every week. Have a soak and stroll in the park and then indulge yourself in a relaxing day in your pyjamas, or do anything else which brings back the happiness that you felt when you looked at the world from a new perspective. Create a mud cake if it is necessary to detach and keep your mind active.

When you exercise, you gain confidence by listening to yourself and trusting in your own abilities as you're aware of the ideals for you and your family. Naturally, you are able to listen to the opinions of others However, only one advice is vital: your own. The process can be challenging to do, but you could collaborate with a partner or an advisor you trust.

All of this has to be grounded in actuality, which means you'll need to be a part of your everyday life. However, how difficult is it to contemplate what you offer to others? The evenings of your week could be yours, or a on a Saturday afternoon.

The practice of yoga can free you from self-criticism

Yoga is a science that helps you live a healthy, balanced mental and physical living. Self-criticism and self-love are two opposing forces, yet most people get punished quickly for making mistakes. We all seem to have a tendency of analyzing our shortcomings all the time.

In the event that no one of us is flawless, it won't be beneficial to keep track of self-esteem frequently. The act of looking at one another is a great way to encourage self-criticism. You may be able to instruct a person to not criticize us However, our minds can be a harbinger of self-criticism anytime during the day. Yoga meditation can aid in training our minds to be less swayed?

Self-criticism can be addressed with a yoga practice.

Swami Kripalu, a twentieth-century spiritual teacher and well-known yoga instructor, once said "The highest form of spiritual practice is self-critical observation." Certain disciplines make it easier for participants to look at themselves from the inside as well as out, just like the ancient practice of meditation. The perennial issue is "who am I?" The answer is self-perception however the process of self-acceptance is more difficult.

The ability to make well-informed decisions demands an enlightened mind and a sense of objectiveness and clarity. But, unreasonable expectations and perfectionist tend to block imagination, diminish self-confidence and cause angry and frustrated. The desire to conform to the norms of someone else, and the way to judge its accomplishments through external praise and insisting on irreproachable results, has opened the way to damaging internal dialog.

Prevention through yoga

If the goal of yoga practice is to bring about a peace between outer and inner spirit, there are a variety of practical ways that may be able to stop the nagging inner voice from becoming impossible to control. In the beginning, however it's crucial to be aware of the phenomenon at its earliest stages. The first signs could be an ache in your throat, tight muscles jaws that are clenched, or any other signs of emotional or physical. Meditation is a method that lets you observe and alter these negative thoughts.

Five strategies to stop self-criticism in the early stages

Take a listen to the songs that resonate with you. If you find your mind filled with negative thoughts, just stop and consider whether it is true. Being aware is the first step in introducing the change.

If you're shocked while watching your critical thoughts make sure to replace the false claims by positive ones.

Perform yoga poses (asanas) to let go of the stagnant energy and cleanse your mind.

Learn techniques for controlled breathing (pranayama).

Write about your emotions. The results of studies have proven that students who suffer from anxiety-related behaviours score higher on tests if they begin writing about their fears.

Chapter 5: Importance Of Self-Criticism

What can you do to make self-criticism work for the success of your business?

Self-criticism can be described as a reflexive assessment and an attitude of criticism towards yourself, your thoughts about your thoughts, beliefs, behavior, your actions and the results you get from them. Self-criticism may be at the root of its growth or decline, based on the usage made of it. We are going to discuss it in this article.

When we take a close review of self-criticism, you will discover the positive as well as negative aspects. This is why I'll explain it using an illustration.

Let's say that I created the wooden toys. It's not the most gorgeous toy available out there. Furthermore, in several ways the toys are unattractive. What can we do to use self-criticism for this?

I am able to see what don't like about the toys and make improvements to the look of toys to come (use self-criticism in order to improve it for the future),

I am embarrassed since I created an ugly toy, and I feel that it is awful as well as ugly. I'm an idiot that doesn't know what to do to create a toy (use self-criticism in order to generate emotions negativity).)

We can, in essence, utilize self-criticism to help us in our next development. Self-criticism may harm us if the value we place on ourselves depends on the things we judge. It is not a good idea to allow the value of his life to be eroded by continuously self-criticism. There is more to life than this.

The pace of change is rapid and our lives have never been more busy than now, and that is one of the main reasons why we should be able to control our self-reflection. What are the advantages of self-reflection? What can I do to help myself reach my goals as well as my next year?

Bad or good?

In the past, self-reflection has been criticized and has shown us that being focused on oneself causes harm and can lead to narcissism. It is the result of my previous attitude regardless of the circumstance of the person. The only difference is the way of thinking, self-criticism as well as the self-reflection, differ. The focus is on the outside of oneself and the outside world. Self-criticism however takes it a step further through examining your own activities from a critical point of view. However, there's no assessment or application. It's just what is not working regardless of what's taking place beneath it. The surface is as we are not sunk and don't fill the empty space. It is crucial to bear the fact that things do sometimes not go as per the plan. However, it's still important to know why or how things go wrong because every failure provides an opportunity to gain knowledge about, enhance and implement various strategies and much more. The money

It can take a long time.

Self-reflection can help you make the time needed to speed up your life. stop and reflect on the present and where you want to go and the things you're doing. Most of the time, we don't take the time to reflect on the place we're at in our lives and without self-reflection we'll never achieve the goals we have set for ourselves and consequently it is possible to follow the path that you don't even think about.

The process of thinking creates consciousness.

Self-reflection helps you fulfill the desires of life, and also creates consciousness. The majority of our dreams don't get realized due to the lack of reflection or awareness. In order to increase the chances in achieving your goals you must be conscious of the current habits of behavior and how they impact on your progress or avoiding these. Reflection on yourself uncovers the contradiction between one's actual state and its objectives that is vital to improving one's self-awareness.

Excellent motivational speaker

Self-reflection causes temporary pain or fear of grieving which could be due to realizing the gap between the current situation and our desired state. Fear of pain can be the driving factor that keeps us going and helps us reach our targets. The pain or sting that is associated with the deviance of a person plays vital roles in making the change in behavior. Self-reflection extends beyond the mere acknowledgment of weaknesses or moments of failing. It is more of an examination of the circumstances that led to the failure, and then focusing on what was done, what he was feeling and what he learned from his experience and the way he plans to move further and make changes to his actions for the future.

The time I spend reflecting has led to moments of awe and remembrance. It's a crucial and integral element of my development team. Every time I perform I take a moment every day to think about and consider whether I'm aligned with my visions and objectives. I think it's crucial to reflect on my goals and thoughts as the reflections that I have made gave me answers about the next steps I need to take in order to achieve my objectives.

Self-reflection is the art of reflection.

Take the initiative to start today to incorporate self-reflection techniques within your everyday routine. Set aside 15 minutes each early morning or in the evening at a minimum three times during the week, but not always daily. Locate a calm place in which where you can sit and reflect and begin to focus on the breath. It is vital to relax your body for a short time to ponder the events that took place in your life and concentrate on the three.

Consider if the events such as projects, assignments, as well as your daily routine give you satisfaction. fulfillment. In any case, there are others like you. A majority of us fill our lives with obligations, and take an keen interest in examining how their actions contribute to the achievement of a larger target, reaching goals or living a goal or a. It is a distraction from pondering your experiences as well as removing the areas which have a negative impact or make you unhappy.

Consider what I have done today to help me achieve my objectives and hopes. The little tasks which are routinely done which will help you attain your goals, and achieve amazing success when the majority of people aren't able to reach them due to the fact that they're not smashed into tiny fragments. If you are thinking of small concrete steps, or even the lack of action the individual focuses on bigger objectives and shifts his focus to smaller tasks in the day which serve a greater objective. A thoughtful and insightful question can help you to focus on the tiny actions you've taken or don't do correctly and allows you to fix the issues for the future.

Think about what I change tomorrow in order to reach my goals? It is important to recognize that everybody gets off the road in some way However, the secret to reaching one's goal isn't to consider these times as an end-to-end failure rather a problem, or a short-lived period. When you think about the question above, you're altering your attitude towards failure in how you approach your problems differently.

How to Build Self Confidence in Your Child?

Perhaps the greatest gift you can offer to your kids is to help your children in developing self-confidence. Confidence in themselves is a must in order to lead an enjoyable and successful life. If they don't have it, they'll always have to fight. However, helping people build confidence in themselves and develop a positive self-esteem might be simpler to say than do. However, don't despair. There are plenty of things to do.

What ever the situation is with your children's needs, you'll be able to start tackling things right now right now, helping your child in creating a sense of certainty. The first thing to do is, on possibility that you're the parent that is attentive to your child, stop and take a break! One of the primary ways to help a child create a sense of confidence and accomplishment is by allowing the child to accomplish tasks independently.

Encourage your child to build confidence in himself by giving them activities that are appropriate for your child's age.

As an example, your six-year-old daughter isn't old enough to contemplate preparing dinner however she is able to assist you in making a couple of desserts. Put the flour into a bowl and mix it up. You can also help her set the ingredients on the sheet. Make her feel empowered at every step and praise her for it. Do not be apprehensive in the event that she creates a mess (acknowledge the possibility that she could!). Additionally, notice how excited she feels at the time when the food is finished! You will be amazed due to the fact that she made them.

When your child is becoming more settled, continue to give her the most challenging tasks and responsibilities. Be aware that she is likely to make mistakes. This is how the way your child is taught. Be sure to praise her progress effectively, while using mistakes as teaching opportunities. Don't be a scolding or reprimanding her for not executing the tasks correctly. It will only hurt her confidence and discourage to her to try again. The confidence she has will grow each time she achieves a feat. Additionally, she will appreciate the love you show, your support, and direction!

Self-criticism can be used to stimulate the growth

It has been observed many times before in publications however, it's worth noting each time. Growing is the goal that all people on Earth is striving for, until they reach the age of adulthood. been able to follow the natural course of development until puberty. It's also a mental and physical growth. For proof, look up an essay from your high school. Take a look now and I'm betting you won't think about how bad your reasoning or style of writing is, or how terrible your writing style is. The way you write has changed over time and your writing skills have improved thanks to the comprehension-enhancing studying you've done in the past, your mind is generating new thoughts and even different ways of thinking and thinking or perhaps your imagination has grown. Whatever the case may be, all indicate growth. The signs are less obvious than physical development, however it is evident that variations are consistent between a couple of years ago and today.

When you reach the age of adulthood the growth rate becomes less normal. This doesn't mean that the world tells you to slow down your growth. In the present, you're an independent individual that can increase your growth rates, and especially mental. Now you're the captain of your vessel and are ruled by only your gut and the decisions you make. Follow the boat to where you would like to travel, and as you go through it, you have the ability to push yourself to stop. Always strive to improve and improve on the one you were before.

Self-criticism happens when the mind naturally recollects. Each time you take a step you take on, your mind is a critique of the act, analyzing it and permitting you to evaluate its origin or, at the very least, what you were feeling from your point viewpoint. While self-reflection can be helpful to develop as a person however, it also can harm the person you are. Your thoughts can bring your body to the floor and begin to hit the ground.

Manage your inner critic and make use of it for your benefit. Allow your brain and self-reflecting conscience judge you as the very best, but do not make yourself feel less confident in yourself. Self-criticism is free. It is the only critique which makes you feel authentic and true as every critic's opinion can be altered by another element which has been altered. Whatever the case, you must acknowledge the criticism accepted, but don't avoid your self-criticism, and allow the accumulation of it and not in a way that causes it to collapse. The process of developing with criticism doesn't mean you are an easy task. That is, you must be truthful, while using this criticism to learn or encourage about yourself.

The aim is to achieve an equilibrium between low and high standards. It is not a good idea to find yourself at one end or the other and instead, be somewhere in between in which you've got the correct guidelines and a clear objective. Don't aim high enough to be able to see the ball, or focus too low, bounce, and strike. If you're prepared to do this, you'll have a better chance to remain on the right path, and you'll have a route that won't be retraced and not chase your.

Chapter 6: To Know Yourself

You are not the only one being mortal it's only your body. The mind is the true you.

Every one of us is an individual. There are different bodies, and abilities, but you're unique.

Your being, however, is not something that is perceived or felt in the external world. There is no fixed condition which doesn't change. It's the way in that you go through your day. The process evolves over the course of your lifetime. This is beyond the structure of your body (which is often surpassed by the natural components). The pattern goes beyond the parts that make up it like you recognize your face as having a pattern that extends beyond the eyes, nose and mouth. It's just as a tune that you are able to comprehend the meaning. But, since it is comprised of numerous facets, it is possible to experience your self through specific parts of it but not the complete. This means that it is impossible to experience every aspect of your self at the simultaneously. But, their psychological comfort as well as their psychological stability are dependent on their understanding that they are the complete person.

The most effective way to visualize the image of yourself is to create an image in your mind by drawing its components: your personality as well as yours. He talks to me and I'm a rare word. There are no synonyms for them.

Me and me are a reference to the parts of yourself which are separate from you. Place yourself in the position of yourself. You are my person and you are the mind as well as your self-awareness.

Your being (your person)

I am the physical manifestation of your personality along with your talents and character that define you as an individual. Present your image to the eyes of other people and your own appearance, as well as their actions. It is the only aspect of you that you look at in the mirror. I am with you on the outside.

The essence of your being is manifested into your conscious by sensory perception of the external environment, your emotions and physical sensations as well as the instinctive bodily images and impulses. Your soul is a reservoir of the desire for pleasure in the physical world, safety and strength. So, their individual preference is to use others to satisfy their needs, and escape or fight whenever their personal requirements are not met. The ego is the "false self" that you have learned to conform to the needs of other people. The"false self" will be identified later.

Even though your nature would like to safeguard your existence but it is not able to rely on me to ensure the happiness of your existence. You may also cause trouble with you, by requesting unattainable protection, a dull lifestyle as well as battling with your peers to control and power, as well as encouraging you to take impulsive decisions.

Your being (your mind)

I am your spirit. Your picture is the mental image you have of your inner and outer realms. It is comprised of your conscious and subconscious ideas and your imagination, as well as your thoughts, your experiences as well as your awareness. These include their opinions, their beliefs and self-conceptions, as well as their perceptions of their particular qualities and opinions on other people.

Your true self

The core of your lies is your intense love and creativity that is your real self.

Your DNA is your authentic self. This is your potential genetic. It's the source of your creative abilities and the one who observes your sexual observations and the location of your thoughts. It's the foundation of your capacity for unconditional love and your honesty skills. the ability to judge honesty, beauty, and justice; the capacity to be morally guilt-ridden and the self-esteem you have. This is your true self!

Your true self-identity is dependent on establishing what could appear to be a slight distinct between sensual and nonsensual words. This distinction, however, is vital to understand the senses that you have in determining your own identity. The reason is that your way to the person you truly are via your sensuality.

To truly understand the distinction between sensual and passionate, it is possible to challenge your own way of being to see the world.

Unfortunately, the society we live in doesn't help you to understand the pleasures of sensuality. One of the major issues that our society faces today is that it's difficult to differentiate between thrilling and sensual experience. This can be seen most distinctly in the confusion about the definition of love. Does love refer to something that's sexual (physical) or a luxurious (spiritual) sensation? It's not a coincidence that the ambiguity of the nature of our love is a reflection of the complexity we are as we don't recognize the difference between sensational experiences from thrilling ones.

The process of establishing and sustaining an exhilarating feeling of yourself isn't straightforward in the modern world that does not promote reverence for the natural rhythms of life as well as pleasures and awkwardness. We are concerned with the sensual stimulation and alleviation of the discomfort of machines, machine-made objects and commercially-produced events from the outside world. In the end, we feel that the goods we purchase have a superior quality to the thrilling experiences we experience on a regular basis in our lives. We invest money, often extravagantly, in search of happiness that money can't buy. We encourage films, TV as well as computers to bring us satisfaction and enjoyment instead of relying on our creative side.

Our culture encourages our satisfaction by immediate pleasures, rather than enjoying the pleasure of sensual pleasure. The goals of commercial and political life are achieved through stifling the physical urges of our bodies. Attracting our fears, desires and pains is an effective method to influence individuals to reach their goals and purchase their goods. Our lives are constantly bombarded by sensory stimulation from the happenings from our external worlds. It's difficult to live calmly about our inner lives.

In the end, people become bored easily and are constantly seeking stimulation through hobbies, work and even chemicals. We all indulge our desires for pleasure, like drinking, smoking, eating as well as excessive sexuality. Our culture is conditioned to want satisfaction in our bodies. This is good for business.

In light of the sexual orientation in our culture In the midst of our society's sensual orientation, you might not be aware of the main distinction between the sense of beauty and sensuality for you, and the physical feeling of sensuality as the bodily pleasure you feel. -Even. However, you are able to understand the distinctions. If you are ruled by your senses and your entire life is centered about how you appear before others, and maintaining your ideal public image. When you're at ease with your sexuality and your inner world, you react to the events of your personal world and your entire life revolves around faith. Sensualisation is her forte. an inclination towards material things and her ability to be sensual helps her develop an inner direction to grow.

Although you may not be aware of it however, once you've experienced the world of your mind, that's where your imagination is rewarded such as when using tools in the field of art or business. The satisfaction of suffering through the result of a thought or action can be a pleasure. While tools can enhance your creativity, they also limit it. using your hands and senile Machines can also replace or increase your ability to think creatively. Computers, for instance, can do the work for you, just as machines do, however they also can help you enhance your creative abilities as tools.

That brings us back to the core of your being. Psychologist Abraham Maslow described actual being as the source of most exciting sensations of the aesthetic in the form of beauty, truth and justice. It is also a source of coherence, simpleness and creativity. The connection to your inner self can be achieved through the delicate feelings like inner peace, motivation confidence, honesty, and effortless efforts. Being authentic is accomplished through the unwavering love for others as well as harmony between conflicts and differences. If you can find the peace of who you are, you will discover the truths that lie in the most fundamental contradictions of the world.

In particular, two intense feelings of moral guilt as well as self-confidence are the two most important factors for expressing who you are. We all are innately able to be afflicted with guilt if we fail to realize or acknowledge our full potential. The thump of guilt although unpleasant, could indicate growth which shows that you and I may not fully comprehend the possibilities of the person we are. Moral guilt, in addition to the social guilt which comes from our consciences of individuals, is healthy and track its effects upon our life. It is a way to enhance our lives.

There is significant distinctions between the romantic and the sensual, there's an essential distinction between what we must do and the things we must perform by executing things as per the expectations of other people. Your inner voice tells you when you should and shouldn't do. disclose its roots by the standards of others. Your values that you acquire from other people are both correct but they are also wrong. Social guilt is a result of your conscience. You may are resentful for being unable to do what you ought to perform, for instance, taking part in a certain religious ceremony. Because it is not inherently ours, we are prone to respond in an uneasy approach. This can cause us to be a victim and create an unproductive depression because we see ourselves as flawed to the gaze of other people and therefore within our own minds. This social guilt could be too high and can hinder our spiritual growth.

However, doing the things we're supposed to be doing is an ethical obligation. Moral guilt reminds us what we are supposed to and shouldn't be doing. Moral guilt reminds us that we're not perfect and we could improve. Inspire the growth of our spiritual lives.

A feeling of confidence in yourself is another sign that you're connected with who you truly are. Self-esteem is when you are proud of your own worth, you develop your strengths and acknowledge your shortcomings. Self-esteem is felt as you assess your own worth and acknowledge the flaws you have.

The real us are part of our community, and they possess the inherent talents of each one of us. These are the genesis of our creative abilities. Although we may not be able to understand our loyal family members completely, these can be exciting zones of constant exploration all through our life. We will discuss our struggles and happiness in our lives.

Your true self

"A busy life can be a life that leads to such a complete identification with the no that there is no one left to die" Bernard Berenson

The newspaper we read in our local published couple of days ago an article called "What is the price of well-being?"

The section states that some of the counties around are named as having the most affluent, with having the highest house prices and the one with the highest amount of foreclosures and bankruptcies. The idea behind the report was that we're often required to keep a certain level of confidence which could lead to the over-expansion of our finances. It was noted that at times the person is so identified as his home or what is to hand which makes it impossible to get rid of these items regardless of whether the financial circumstances change.

The journalist who wrote the piece interviewed a man, who just quit his job, and was embarrassed to own an Volvo instead of an Mercedes. The columnist was told that he didn't want people to think that he was driving around in a less costly car. He believes that his identity is derived from objects. This is what Deepak Chopra describes in his book "reference to an object" The seven laws of the spiritual for success.

Quoted by Chopra: "About objects, your internal point of reference is your ego, but the ego is not what it is, the ego is your trust, ... your social mask; the role you play. " The social mask is successful with approval. The person should be governed because he's fearful of appearing less than the other. But the pure white (mind/soul) doesn't feel less or more superior since your true self appears to be identical.

If the identity you have is derived from the name, location or size of your home or the number on your home, it's an untrue power or state. The identity of the object that is referenced is valid as long as the object remains there. What happens when the property, title or item disappears? Does that mean your identity has disappeared? NO! Since your real you does not change. The beauty you truly possess is eternal natural, untamed and lovable. When you describe yourself as an independent person (of your true self) then you're attracted by the attention of people, occasions and supporters in expressing your wishes and ambitions. It is not a struggle to keep objects or things.

What do you consider to be what is currently your source of personal identity? Are you concerned that other people aren't happy with it or think they aren't a part of it "if they do not wear" appropriate clothing "or do not drive a" genuine vehicle "? Think about:" If I lost my job or property quickly whom would it be? What am I today and what's my goal? "Take the time to consider these issues and sit in quiet throughout the day. It is the most effective method to discover your authentic person!

False selfies

As the early Greek performers wore masks throughout the stage performance, we have used our covers as fake characters to save photographs of the world which we've learned to display in various identities. One obvious instance is when we approach our work in different ways as our families who live at home. The way we think about ourselves is based on these wrong beliefs that we acquired at first during our childhood the roles we played. Therefore, we do and say the things we are required to do our behavior in social settings. What parts of us show to other people belong to us.

Our fake creatures manifests themselves through their behavior of maintaining a certain appearance in the eyes of other people. The people who are dishonest require an adjustment in their social lives since there are reasonably high expectations of others. In reality the best way to shop is to shop when managers of stores act mannerly, even when they're exhausted and excited to get to their homes. We suggest avoiding the false image during social interactions.

The phrase "false self" is an accurate description of one of our exterior faces because it's in accordance with the notion that we are both imperfect humans who are constantly striving to understand and show our authentic selves within the world. Social housing is essential for you. This term can also help clarify why I and you frequently feel as if we are fakes and the reason why certain of us are referred to as "fake". This is the challenge of his and my mission in every aspect to become as true as possible messages to the fake ones.

This task becomes more challenging. Technology advancements and the changes to our lifestyles in the past century provide us with a variety of new roles in society. One consequence of this overstimulation in the social sphere has been the creation of characters that appeal to ever more people including fathers in-law, father, son, father-in-law brothers, husbands former husband, student friend, teacher or sportsperson, friend, colleague. Customer, seller an employee, boss taxpayer voter, critic, translator protector, pastor driver, traveler, associate with, author, the victim, writer or adoptive father, son, adoptive father, foster child and the list goes on after. It is evident that every one of these roles concentrates on different aspects of who you are.

Are you aware that the characters you perform add anxiety within your own day-to-day life? Doesn't this seem to be the case in the event that the motive to play the role comes from outside rather than from the internal world?

Our illusions of being built on our perceptions and the perception of others. They can be defined by what we can and cannot perceive, hear, and feel. They are inextricably linked to our real physical existence. An individual who has a problem generally appears to conform to our expectations of what other people have about us. This can, however, be a sign of rebellion against other expectations like a rebellious teenager is. It could be in response to the way other people view you, just like a shy person. It is also possible to hide undesirable aspects of yourself, just as is the case with a religious person. False self-images are also vulnerable to breakdowns when "others do not look at it".

The false self lacks authenticity because it is defined by social norms as well as our mental mechanisms for protection. It is not influenced the real us. They tend to adopt traits of an individual with expectations that are established or interpreted differently. Therefore, we may have mixed opinions about the false self. They could either go beyond what others expect or differ from the expectations of other. That's why we might be conflicted concerning our roles in the context of prayer and the relationships with our families. It is possible that we are uncertain about what other people would like from us, since it isn't clear to other people what they want from us.

Our false selves can make us confused and destroy relationships if the real us do not make or maintain their own relationships. When the people we are dishonest with do not connect with our true human beings, we're like machines that replicate the recorded messages to conform to the expectations of others in certain phases of our lives. The fake people we hire can be inflexible and incapable of adapting to the changing roles in society. This is why we are at risk of changes, but we are able to stick with our rigid belief systems and theories that believe to be right.

Chapter 7: What Is Perfectionism?

The people who are perfectionists adhere to extremely strict requirements. They feel that the work they do isn't enough.

A few people are mistakenly under an assumption that perfectionists are an effective motivator. However, this isn't the case. Perfectionists can leave you unhappy with the way you live your life. This could lead to an anxiety-based depression, stress as well as eating disorders as well as injuries. It could also deter people from attempting to achieve success. A few minor instances of perfectionists may negatively impact your life. It can affect your relations, work or studies.

Perfectionionism is a problem for young people as well as older adults as well. Teens and children are typically motivated to achieve the highest levels when it comes to schoolwork, and other activities such as clubs, sports as well as community service and work. This may lead to obsessiveness that ultimately could hinder the ability of a person to attain achievement.

ARE YOU A PERFECTIONIST?

If you're asking yourself if you're a perfectionist most likely you're at a certain degree. If we're being honest you have the possibility that you believe in the image as a perfectionist due to it has positive associations that come with the term "Perfect": who doesn't desire to achieve perfection in addition to feeling great? (Perfectionists, that's who!)

It is crucial to educate yourself about what is considered perfectionists and why it's thought to be a sin to determine how hard you would like to do in removing this type of behavior and the best way to achieve it.

The issue with perfectionists and the reason why you'd like to find out whether you are a perfectionist and the best way to combat it is because those who excel tend to achieve little and have more stress than normal high-achieving people.

They are very similar to the high-achieving, they have some distinct differences which are significant since perfectionists are more likely to be more stressed.

The following are the ten most revealing attributes of perfectionists. These traits may observe in yourself or among people you've met. Are any of these familiar?

All-or-Nothing Thinking

The best, as well as the perfectionists have a tendency to set lofty objectives and put in the effort in order to attain these goals. A successful person might be content with his excellent work and the achievement of excellence (or some similar thing) regardless of whether his goals do not get fulfilled. They will not settle for less than the highest level of perfection. "Almost perfect" is considered to be a fail.

Critical eye

Perfectionists tend to be more criticizing themselves and other people more than those who achieve high levels. High achievers can be proud of their achievements and often to encourage their peers, perfectionists often find small flaws and errors both in their work and in the work of others. They are adamant about these flaws and are unable to see any other flaws, and tend to be more demanding and harsh on the other people around them when they've "failed."

"Push" vs. "Pull"

Highly successful people are drawn towards their goals because of their desire to achieve them and feel satisfied with their efforts to get there. However those who are perfectionists will be driven towards their goals due to the fears of failing to achieve the goals they set and consider anything that isn't a perfect target as failing.

Standards that aren't realistic

The goals of perfectionists aren't necessarily attainable. Although high-level performers can establish their objectives and set them to a high standard, they may also appreciate having fun making new goals, and then going in the same direction after the goals have been achieved. But the perfectionists usually put their original targets out of reach and are unable to enjoy their journey.

Highly accomplished people are generally happy and more productive than those who strive to be perfect in their pursuit of targets.

Concentrate on the Results

Highly successful individuals understand the importance of working towards a goal in addition to the accomplishment of their target. However, people who strive to be perfect only focus on the objective only as a goal. They're so focused on reaching their goal and avoid the fear of failing that they are able to appreciate their progress and are fully engaged with the procedure.

Affected by goals missed

They are far less satisfied and relaxed than high performers. High achievers are able to recover from failure with ease however, perfectionists are more likely to argue a lot more, and indulge in hurt feelings whenever they don't get their goals fulfilled.

Be afraid of making a mistake

The perfectionists are less scared of failing than they are of success. As they are so invested in their results, and they are satisfied with only perfect, failing becomes an extremely frightening possibility. Like everything else that isn't the perfect result is seen as to be a failing, those who strive for perfection often postpone things to the very last moment.

Procrastination

It's not surprising that those who excel at their craft are more likely to delay and this could affect productivity. But the two tend to be inextricably linked. It is because, because from fear of failing to do things right, perfectionists can are so worried about making an imperfect task that they just are unable to do everything.

The act of putting off work can cause a deeper sense of failing, further sustaining an unending and crippling cycle.

Defensiveness

Since performance that is perfect can be difficult and frightening for those who are those who are perfectionists, they often dismiss criticism constructively High achievers might view criticism as constructive as a way to improve their performance. better.

Self-esteem is low.

The people who excel naturally have a high self-esteem, but this does not apply to people who strive to be perfect. They tend to be extremely unsatisfied and critical, and are afflicted with poor self-esteem. They are also often left by themselves or alone because of their severe nature and inflexibility could cause others to feel resentful. It can result in low self-esteem.

WHY YOU SHOULD STOP TRYING TO BE PERFECT - BENEFITS OF IMPERFECTION

Are you setting your targets each day to ensure that all is in order? Did you reach minimum half of your set goals you've set? Don't worry. It's not all your fault. There are many that are flawed.

It is impossible to alter anything in your existence if you choose not to follow through with what was legally required. The only thing you have to accept that you're not perfect.

It is possible that you have stopped adhering to an ideal diet because you've cheated a couple of times or you quit going to the gym because you were unable to go into the fitness center for a couple of days, or quit dating someone simply because the person you are dating isn't flawless? The reason is due to the pressure to achieve perfection.

Never pressurize or make yourself feel pressured to do anything because the pressure can lead to failing and dissatisfaction.

So, the most effective way to approach this is stop attempting to be perfect, and instead accept your imperfections. You are human. There are many advantages of being both imperfect and ideal for learning through being flawed.

Here are the major benefits derived from imperfections ...

It is possible to maintain a certain weight if you're not attempting to lose weight. When you decide to reduce weight or diet but you might not adhere to these exact and quick regulations. If you do fall short once in a while and feel you're being a success. Why are you striving to achieve perfection? It is not necessary to achieve perfection by adhering to an exact eating plan. Instead, try eating as healthful as you can.

If you're unable to accomplish things, acknowledge it and seek assistance. If you are honest about your shortcomings and ask for help, you'll be able to establish a more enduring relationship with your loved ones, family members, or even your partners. Inquiring for help is not an admission of weakness. It acknowledges that you're a human being, and it shows your vulnerability, which can aid others who are in your position.

It is natural to explore new possibilities in the absence of striving to achieve perfection. When, for example, you are unable to make it work with a particular project it is possible to improvise and claim that you did something similar, only this time with an entirely new method. If you aren't able to do it correctly, you will try to think differently until you force yourself to make it better.

Accept the mistakes of others if you recognize that you're not the perfect person. When you learn in your growth, progress, and get better, you will want to be the best for others. When you recognize the difficulty of trying to attain perfection and realize the fact that there is no such thing then you'll be able to empathize and understand other people and be able to accept their shortcomings.

The first time you will start to appreciate yourself once you realize the fact that you're not flawless. When you're inadequate, it might not be simple to move toward your goals and complete every task until everything is perfect scheduled, or when you've got everything together. But once you acknowledge where you are with everything the imperfections you've got, your imperfections and beauty, you will begin to appreciate your self by doing some things each day.

Accepting the imperfections of your life in the process of achieving the goals you have set can cause you to smile as you consider your previous. True, since the moment you realize the fact that you're not perfect but continue to achieve your objectives, you will are able to become better versions of you over the course of time. There's nothing as being perfect. You just become an improved version of yourself that you were. The errors you have made in the process will provide you with some lessons, or even good memories that bring you to laughter.

Therefore, even though there are many benefits having imperfections in your life and learning new the things around your life, why do attempt to achieve perfection? The imperfections you make can help you to lead a healthier life, healthier and more enjoyable lifestyle than you do when you try to be perfect.

Don't let your life be focused on the things you aren't able to accomplish all at once. Continue to learn, try to become an improved version of yourself and you'll soon be "perfect". Enjoy your not-so ideal life!

Chapter 8: Overcoming Perfectionism - What You Can Do

Are you a perfectionist? A lot of people exhibit perfectionist characteristics and feel proud of their achievements However, there are some important differentiators between perfectionists and the high-achieving, and having a higher level of achievement will benefit the health of your body and well-being. If you are prone to perfectionist traits It is crucial to discover ways to conquer the urge to be a perfectionist. Perfectionist tendencies can deprive the person of their satisfaction, happiness as well as self-esteem. Though it's an exhausting and time-consuming method, the process of shedding the weight of perfection can dramatically decrease the anxiety you feel every day.

IMPORTANT DISTINCTIONS BETWEEN PERFECTIONISTS AND HIGH ACHIEVERS

Prior to focusing on ways to overcome perfectionist tendencies, it's important to be aware of the fundamental principles of what perfection is and not. this will allow you to stay inspired to change your habits. The concept of perfectionism is different from that of high-achieving people in a fundamental way, namely how much attention you pay to. If you're seeking perfection, you will feel satisfied with the results and gain knowledge from mistakes.

It is different from other types of perfectionists because it is not as tolerant. Those who are perfect struggle for every thing that appears to be lacking, which reduces the joy and joy that is derived from their accomplishments. One of the main issues that perfectionists have to face is that they fear by letting go of the pursuit of the highest standards, they'll become poor performers and their objectives are not achieved. I want to assure you that abandoning perfectionist mindsets helps to make you stand out!

In the meantime, here are some steps that you can adopt to ensure an upbeat, healthy mindset.

LETTING GO OF THE ALL-OR-NOTHING MINDSET

A "all or nothing" mentality is an important issue among people who are perfectionists generally. Perfectionists think about their lives in terms of extremely rigid distinctions. Like, "Black" or "White." "All or nothing." "Success" or "Failure." "Complete all" or "Do nothing."

This thought, however, can be self-defeating, and in the best case, a lie. In reality everyone fails with no the possibility of failure. Every athlete fails to win a contest in the absence of a struggle with their training. Every entrepreneur fails after failing in one way or the other. It is impossible to create outstanding work without fighting their equipment and resulting in something that isn't good. Actually, all things happen as a process, not in an the all-or-nothing way.

It is evident that this "all or nothing" mindset can lead to unrealistic expectations of us and for others. It can also make us self-critical and harsh on us and other people. The idea of all-or-nothing is common among perfectionists and can be a sign of depression and anxiety.

What can we do to completely alter the idea of everything or absolutely nothing? Here are six methods to start.

1.) Seek out positives.

The tendency is to focus on and recall the negative elements of our lives, such as mistakes and disappointments occasions when events didn't go according to expected. A negative mindset is what makes you recall being late to the most important event and not remember the hundreds of times that you've been in time. It can lead to the thought that all or nothing of "I'm always late" and likely a string of self-critical remarks that criticize one another for doing things that aren't true. This requires a lot of effort and discipline, but it is possible to train yourself to appreciate the good things in your life, the effort you put into it and the things that you are able to learn and the things that you cherish about your self and other people and the little delights that can make your life more enjoyable.

2.) Keep an open mind.

It is possible to expand our thought beyond the dichotomy of either right or wrong, or good or bad, through being a bit interested and challenging our entire or nothing thought. This kind of distorted thinking pattern tends to be well-established and often never even noticeably and we must begin to notice these patterns. When you realise you are thinking about nothing or nothing, you should ask yourself several questions to test your thinking and determine whether there is another way to think about issues. There is a possibility that you are wondering:

Do I put too much pressure on myself (or anyone else)?

Are my expectations realistic?

Do you think this idea helped me?

Are I making up my mind?

Do you have a different way to look at this?

Do you think perfectionists are at work in this case?

Are there positive elements of the development that I am unable to discern?

3.) Create your own thinking process and seek out "shades of gray."

Because all or nothing thinking relies upon unrealistic and absolute expectations, it is best to stay away from saying things like never, must, all one, or all should, all, ought and. Think beyond terms like failure successful, failure, negative and positive look to see whether you can come up with more specific words that do not express these extremes.

4) Authorize paradoxes.

A second option is to recognize the fact that opposites are real, and you don't must choose one or either. As an example, your spouse could be angry and loving. Your work can be monotonous and stressful. It is possible to be innovative and well-organized.

5.) Try to find partial wins.

Instead of basing your decisions in a way that is based on either failure or success instead, consider using the method of partial successes. This article explains how you can look for partial success and advantages of this strategy.

"It's easy to not start something when we believe that they're impossible to accomplish. The kind of "all or nothing" thinking is difficult to comprehend that in most cases, there's the benefit of being a an integral part of a project, or even that some things are not done in a way that isn't up to the highest standards. If I decide to go to the gym each early in the morning, however I took a long time eating breakfast, and there's no chance to attend the class I absolutely love. If my perfectionist thoughts to set in then I'd say "It's already too late. I'm not sure I'll be able to workout this day." In other words I might say, "Well, I missed the spin class but I can still walk for 20 minutes after working." The perfectionist in me would want to consider me an failure since I failed to keep my promise to attend the spin class, and because walking wasn't as effective as an exercise. A more compassionate approach and being willing to contemplate this, which can prevent my from slipping into despair and procrastination later on can be described as a fractional achievement.

"It is extremely difficult to be motivated if you think of things solely in terms of "success" as opposed to "failure." The majority of our lives is actually shades of gray. If we set false expectations on ourselves and feel that we're not good enough (or dumb or incompetent) and the performance of ours isn't perfect It is much easy to ignore it. A short walk is not a great workout however, it did provide me with positive health effects. The same is true for writing down your budget, journaling as well as eating healthy, and anything else that we're attempting to perform. That's why it's not necessary to perform things perfect before they are worth it."

6) Don't let mistakes define you.

The idea of doing the world makes us believe errors are failures, and failing is a fatality. In reality, there are always mistakes to be made; everyone says and accomplishes good things. Most of the top people in the world can say that being disappointed is an essential part of achievement. In the end, at the end of the day, there will experience both a victory and failure - and everything happens in between. Instead of attempting to stay clear of mistakes, recognize and take lessons from them. take them as an opportunity to open opportunities to improve your personal growth.

When you begin to notice that all-or-nothing-thinking starts to creep in, try at the very least one of these methods to confront these thoughts of perfection. In this way, you will create an increase in kindness for yourself and other people throughout your day. It can lead to greater happiness, satisfaction as well as self-esteem.

Chapter 9: Learning To Silence Your Inner Critics And Love Yourself

Since I am a perfectionist, recognize the negative self-talk and self-denial that can occur particularly when situations become challenging. It's not difficult to feel guilty for things that don't go as expected. It's simple to put off your health because you value the work you do. Also, it is easy to take responsibility for others' difficulties and mistakes.

Imagine having a close friend who is extremely critical. He will let you know that you've put on a few pounds. He causes you to lose your confidence prior to a presentation. He reveals your weaknesses and prompts you to admit that you're not performing the same as other people. If you were a close friend such as that, you'd strike him in the face and he would be a screamer, wouldn't you? There is no need for this kind of negative energy in their lives! If we can't take criticism from our peers, then why should we allow it to be a part of us?

We allow ourselves to be surrounded by an enthralling amount of negative remarks. It happens often enough that it becomes background noise. However, the kind of comments you hear will seriously affect confidence in yourself. The question is, what do you do to shut down those who criticize you? Five great suggestions:

1. Pay attention to negative thinking

This may seem counterintuitive it's true that you're able to shut out your inner critics once you recognize it. It is not my intention to feed to it, but instead take the time to consider these voices of negativity from a distance in the best way feasible. The majority of negative thoughts arise out of undeserved anxieties. Spend some time listening to the words you're speaking and discover that your negative comments are usually nonsense. If you would not say something to someone you know then why would you say you would?

2. Be productive

Though many of our negative beliefs can be unjustified and unfairly judged Some of the criticisms are based on real issues which need to be dealt with. If you have areas in your life aren't working Do something about it. Don't give yourself the opportunity to make negative comments about yourself. There's nothing more frustrating than the constant voice that pops into your mind to remind you yet again that you're late. Even if you are aware that the truth, it may result in an endless cycle of critique.

Be mean to yourself unwise and definitely ineffective. Instead, make concrete efforts in order to grow. Make goals and keep track of the progress you make. Even if it's just tiny steps, slowly improving your self-esteem will help change negative thoughts into positive ones, and ultimately eliminate your internal critics.

3. Consider how you view the world around you.

Any negative thoughts will harm your soul. If you let yourself criticize and judge other people (admit it! We've had to be there!) You're merely preparing your self to believe that it's acceptable to judge you. Refrain from gossip and keep away from quick judgments even if they seem innocent. If you are a victim of negativity, it can only be a biting wound in your back.

4. You can ask yourself this question.

Do you know if self-critical? Consider asking yourself: Would you tell your self in five years? Would you inform your five year old self that they're insufficiently intelligent, they're obese or lack ability? No! It is a good idea to tell your children to be confident that they are a person who believes in them and have the power to decide what to accomplish. Therefore, if you're going to not make a negative impression on yourself as a child then why would you today? The self-confidence of a person can be damaged in any stage of life and we must ensure that we are doing all we can to help our self-esteem.

5. Remember that you are incredible

Sometimes, the best method to stifle your inner critic is to drown it out with positive affirmations. It could be as simple as standing the mirror and doing a self-esteem talking and telling yourself positive affirmations are a great way to boost your confidence even when you're feeling really negative. Actually, I have an extra piece of paper in my wallet which highlights my strengths. Every time I begin the negative thoughts I look at my letter and I am reminded of my strength and confidence in my talents. The goal is not to boast or trying to build your self-esteem, it's about expressing your truth about the things you're accomplishing. We all require an occasional reminder of the fact that we're capable individuals capable of handling whatever life requires!

USE YOUR IDEAS AS GUIDES, NOT ABSOLUTES

The perfectionists are often overly attached to their targets. When they fail to achieve an objective? That means they did not succeed; they may think. If they didn't achieve their goal in an appropriate time period? That means they're useless and they are thinking. They view their goals as an indication of their value and get angry when problems arise. Others decide that their goals do not fit their needs and completely avoid setting goals and end up in depression.

Is that really the case? When you aren't able to reach the goals you set (in an efficient manner) is it a sign that you're useless and unworthy? No, of course that's not the case. Even if you didn't achieve your goals within a particular amount of time doesn't mean you're failing simply means that you did not meet your objectives within that particular duration of time. It could be that there were issues which have occurred. Perhaps your method isn't the best one. Maybe the goal you're trying to achieve is not in alignment with your goals and you must define an objective that is more consistent.

Make sure that your objectives are merely guides but not absolutes. "Guide" means that your objective is to direct you along the path of improvements. "It is not absolute" signifies that your objective is not an arduous and unmeasurable one, but failing to achieve it implies that you're a flawed individual (which is, of course would be a huge lie). Your worth is greater than targets and the results. Your goal is to create a massive impact within the entire universe.

That means you must keep setting big goals. Allow your heart to go wild by imagining your ideals and hopes and let them guide your. If you've achieved a particular objective, it's not more important than the fact that you're making progress toward the goal.

Keep in mind that the main aim in life is growth and become the best version of yourself. The goals and objectives you set serve as a guide to assist you to achieve your goals.

CELEBRATE ALL PROGRESS, VICTORY, AND FAILURE

Perfectionists are known to dwell on their shortcomings even though they have excessive expectations for their abilities. They are not satisfied until they've achieved the level they have achieved. They're not always satisfied with their work. They constantly look for problems, mistakes to fix. But they rarely begrudge themselves when they've accomplished well, rather they just take it for to be taken for.

It's probably an aspect of our lives that you experience continual dissatisfaction about your work, and to feel sorrow over it. This helps to focus in constructing new areas with your work and enhancing the gaps in your work. What if I offered an alternative method? You should be celebrating every single thing you've done such as your achievements and achievements, as well as the mistakes you make, as well as your mistakes. Even your errors and failures. That means that if you've "just" progressed by 1 percentage in your job Celebrate the fact that you made progress. If you come across some obstacle, rejoice in your discovery of this obscure area that you didn't recognize prior to. If you've made mistakes take note of them and rectify them. Thank yourself for the improving and gaining knowledge. Rejoice in your successes and give yourself a massive applause to a job well-done.

It's exciting because it is possible that this won't make you more relaxed at work. It actually encourages you to strive for your most effective. It acknowledges your strengths and capabilities and helps you to make the most out of these. This makes your life more enjoyable, exciting and relaxing. Since, in contrast to constant focus on what's not there the present moment, you are aware of the things you already have. A positive, abundant mindset can help to build positivity, self-confidence, and feelings of happiness.

www.ingramcontent.com/pod-product-compliance
Lightning Source LLC
Chambersburg PA
CBHW060222030426
42335CB00014B/1309